# THE ART OF THE

# NEW ZEALAND TATTOO

# THE ART OF THE
# NEW ZEALAND TATTOO

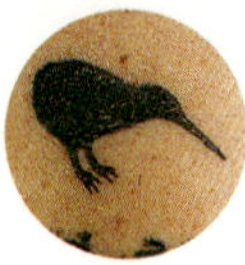

## ANNE NICHOLAS

### FOREWORD BY NIGEL COX

A CITADEL PRESS BOOK

PUBLISHED BY CAROL PUBLISHING GROUP

A Citadel Press Book
Published by Carol Publishing Group

Citadel Press is a registered trademark of Carol Communications, Inc.

Editorial Offices: 600 Madison Avenue, New York, N.Y. 10022
Sales and Distribution Offices:
120 Enterprise Avenue, Secaucus, N.J. 07094
In Canada:
Canadian Manda Group, One Atlantic Avenue / Suite 105, Toronto,
Ontario M6K 3G7
Queries regarding rights and permissions should be addressed to:
Carol Publishing Group, 600 Madison Avenue, New York, N.Y. 10022

Carol Publishing Group books are available at special discounts for bulk purchases,
sales promotion, fund-raising, or educational purposes. Special editions can be
created to specifications. For details, contact: Special Sales Department, Carol
Publishing Group, 120 Enterprise Avenue, Secaucus, N.J. 07094

Published by arrangement with Tandem Press, New Zealand

Manufactured in Hong Kong

10 9 8 7 6 5 4 3 2 1

ISBN 0-8065-1603-8

# CONTENTS

## NIGEL COX

NEAR THE END of Janet Frame's novel *A State of Siege* the novel's heroine, Malfred Signal, dreams she is on a wharf, where she is approached by a tramp. 'Now the hobo, vagrant, call him what you will . . . picks up a discarded cigarette butt and, without a grimace, puts it in his mouth, while I, sitting here so neat, so particular always in my dress and habits, feel a desire to vomit. Where has all our training in public hygiene led us if these nasty old men persist in picking up and smoking cigarette butts?'

The nausea Malfred feels is very like the nausea and disgust many people, neat in their dress and habits, feel when they imagine themselves being tattooed. That the dirt of the world, like a cigarette butt picked up off the ground and put in the mouth, is going to enter the body; and, having once entered, is going to stay, to live in the body, forever; and not only live there, but live there visibly, on the body's surface, where everyone can see: as Kurtz says in *Apocalypse Now*, 'The horror; the horror . . . .'

*Apocalypse Now* stretches back through Conrad's *Heart of Darkness* to the idea that white people (like us) must keep themselves clean of contact with dirty, primitive, primal, black people, who will offer the irresistible temptation of abandoning their duty-bound, monogamous, anal-retentive lives in favour of wild sex, indolence, devil-worshipping and sensuality (amen!). This is what a secretary from one of the more discreet suburbs, neat in dress and habits, hopes to evoke when she gets a small blue butterfly tattooed on her bottom; that the wildness hidden inside her can be brought to the surface. It's why US Secretary of State George Shultz had a tiger's head on his backside. It's what

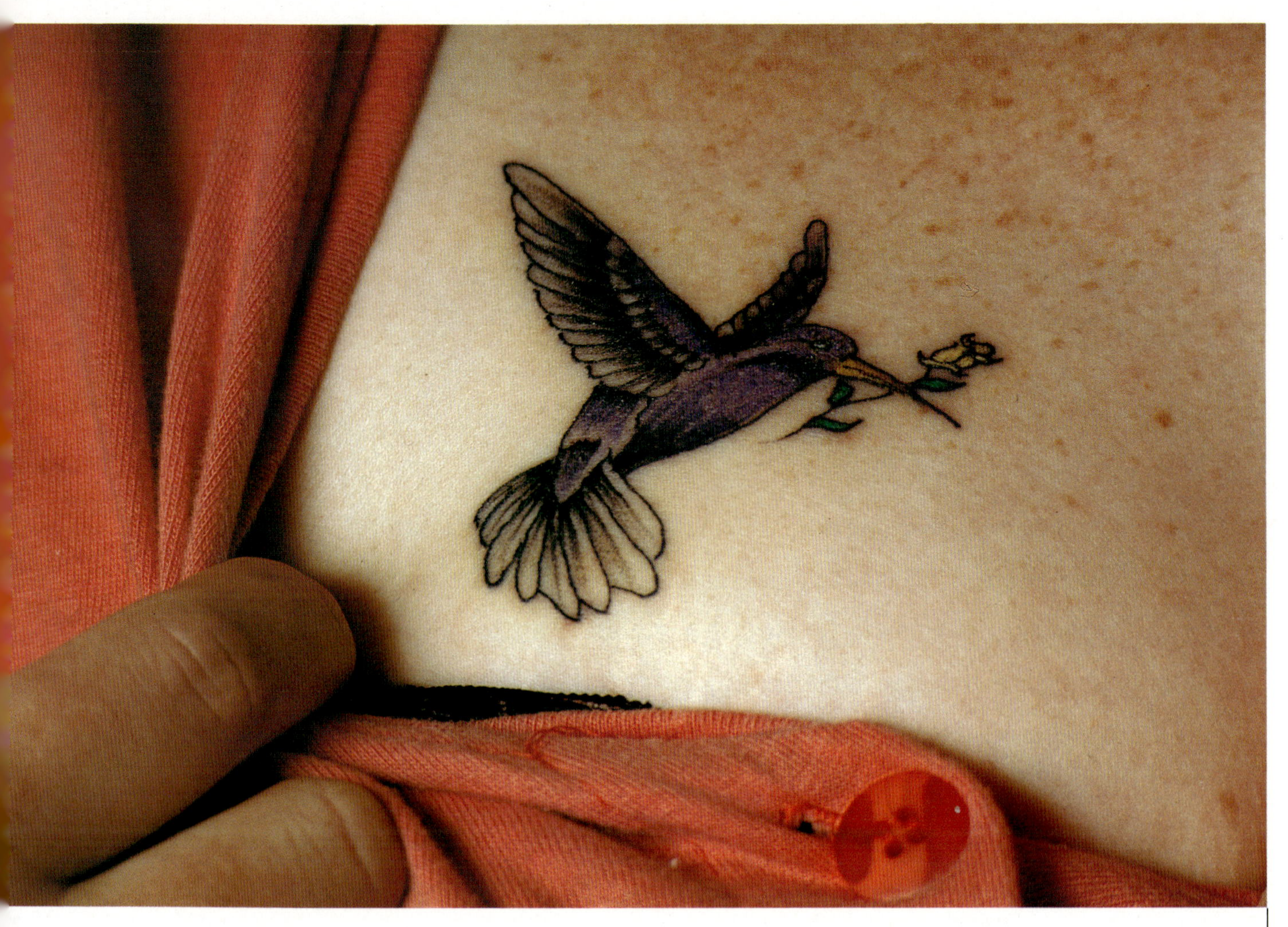



the pop group Red Hot Chili Peppers hope to evoke with the gallery of their tattoos

on the cover of *Blood Sugar Sex Magik*. The modern primitive, the urban(e) animal.

But just as 'primitive' is itself an idea that is slipping from use, so is the practice of

hiding tattoos. These days they are being worn (can you say *worn* of something that

can't be taken off?) where they can be seen. The old designs — 'The sweetest girl I

ever kissed was another man's wife . . . my mother'; snake-and-dagger; the babe that

the bicep wriggles — are being replaced by a new ethos, art. Like everything else in the modern world, tattoo has been going back to its roots, and bringing those influences of origin through to take their place among the images which surround us.

Tattoo's origins lie in antiquity. Mummies from Egypt when unwrapped 4000 years later reveal patterns of dots and dashes beneath the skin, like morse, a communication which reaches across immense distances, in this case, of time: tattoos outlive everything, even the death of the body. In the British Isles both the Picts (the name comes from 'pictured people') and the Celts, who because of their body markings were 'fearful to look upon in battle', according to Julius Caesar, had highly developed traditions of skin pricking. In Borneo, the Americas and in Japan, tribal peoples developed systems of body adornment that were also a kind of language; for example, tattoos on an Iban (Sarawak) chief's hands indicated that he had taken a human head. Perhaps the strongest traditions developed in the South Pacific, where in the warmer climates Polynesian tattooing developed to become what might be regarded as 'clothing that talks'.

Tattooing has always been practised in Europe, in Germany and Gaul, among the Britons and the Thracians, though it was suppressed with the rise of Christianity because of the Bible's admonishments against altering God's handiwork, the body. According to Leviticus, 'Ye shall not make any cutting in your flesh for the dead, nor print any marks upon you.'

IT WAS JAMES COOK as much as anybody who was responsible for the resurgence of European interest in tattooing. The journals which record his voyage to the Pacific include precise descriptions of tattoo-making. 'They stain their bodies by indentings,' Cook wrote, 'or pricking the skin with small instruments made of bone, cut into short teeth; which indentings they fill up with dark blue or blacking mixture prepared from the smoke of an oily nut.' Cook also carried home with him the word which was to become Polynesia's main contribution to the English language. *Tatau*, from the Tahitian for 'to mark', soon replaced the established description, 'pricking'. Cook also took an example of tattoo home with him, in the person of Omai, a Tahitian, who was paraded among the British as a kind of living exhibit — this description insults a man of intelligence and great dignity — and within a few years no circus sideshow was complete without its 'tattooed wildman'. These exhibits, along with other factors (for example the development of the electric tattooing needle patented in 1891), led to the rise of tattooing as a fashion among the stylish and well-bred in the early

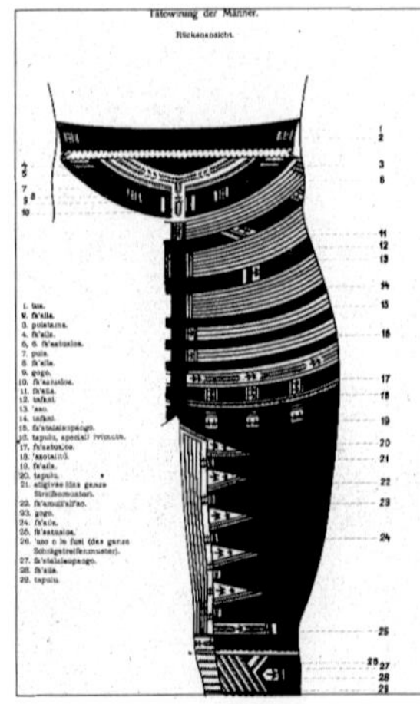

*plate 2*

part of this century. The young prince who was to become King George V had his forearm embellished when in Japan during his time in the navy. Lady Randolph Churchill had a snake with its tail in its mouth tattooed around her wrist, a charm she was careful to hide in the twenties with a bracelet, when tattoos became unfashionable.

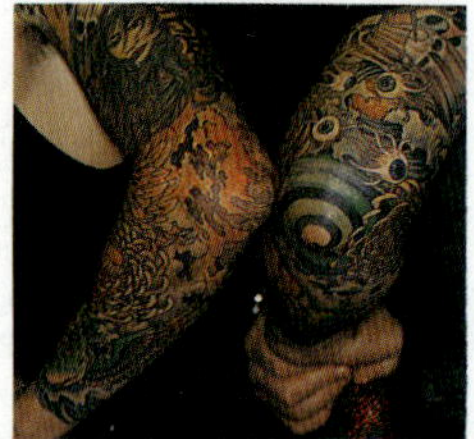



THE WORD TATTOO, now widely used (in Japan, which has a distinct and particularly subtle tradition of its own, the word is *ire-zumi*, for 'the insertion of ink'), and the practice it refers to, spread widely, largely through the enthusiasm and voyaging of sailors. The military, and those who wished to make indelible marks of punishment or demarcation, have used tattoo for centuries. The Nazis numbered the Jews, the military tattooed deserters with the letter 'D', and during the Edo period (1603-1867) the foreheads of Japanese criminals were marked with a line for each crime — a third offence, leading to a third mark, completed the character for the word 'dog'. The idea was taken to its extreme by Kafka, whose story *In The Penal Settlement* describes a machine which repeatedly tattoos a description of the offender's crimes into his skin, going ever deeper, until death results (though, since this is Kafka, the death is one of ecstasy and revelation).

As the century has progressed, however, tattoo among 'Europeans' has gradually shrugged off its lowly origins and aspired to becoming an art form.

It's an art which demands that a remarkable relationship develop between the artists and their 'canvases'. All artists evolve intimate relationships with their materials, but in tattoo the canvas is alive and, since it will walk away bearing the work, must decide what the artwork will depict. Yet the artists are not the tattooed upon, but the tattooers, who, by reputation, earn commissions in a fashion similar to the patronage given to painters in the past. To make his art the tattooist must inflict considerable pain upon his subject and so a particular relationship develops. A client of Samoan tattooist Paulo

Sulu'ape says, 'When I am receiving work from my Tattoo Artist, there is only him and I and the pain.'

Samoan *tatu* is applied by adze-like combs with teeth of bone or boar's tusk which, having been dipped in the ink, are tapped into the skin with a mallet. Two apprentices pull the skin taut, a third dabs the blood away. Prayers are sung constantly to provide an alternative focus to the pain, but after a session lasting four or five hours the recipient can be seen wincing with every stroke. Some tattooists may complete an entire tattoo in several pain-filled days, but others stretch the process out over months. Extending from below the knee to the base of the ribs, the last area to be covered by the tattoo's pattern is the navel, symbolising the cutting of the umbilical cord, or the completion of the walk from boy to man.

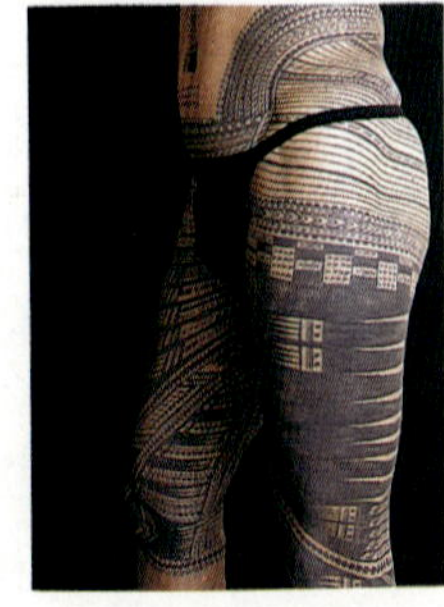

*plate 4*

Samoan tattoo has a living tradition which it has kept free of Western influence. Nevertheless it is influencing the non-Samoan tradition in New Zealand tattooing. A number of palagi have had themselves tattooed Samoan-style (an early recipient was the painter Tony Fomison), and in the fashionable cafés of Auckland's High Street, braidings and comb-patterns can be seen just beyond the margin of shirt sleeves or shorts. Of course, historically, New Zealand tattoo has absorbed the international style of variations on clichéd and formulaic themes (daggers, dragons, dice) which were among the reasons tattoo was held in low regard. But in recent years a new aesthetic has developed, where the tattooists see themselves as artists and aspire to art's rigour. Tattoo is a difficult art to develop; after all, no one wants to wear your failed experiment for the rest of their life. But clear progress has been made, especially in the selection of new and more thoughtfully chosen subject matter, to which the range of photographs in this book attest.

NEW ZEALAND'S TATTOO TRADITION has an influence which is unique and one which is gradually gaining what will undoubtedly prove to be an unshakeable hold on all tattooing done in this country. That influence is the Maori one. Tattoo, called moko by the Maori, played a vital part in the highly evolved pattern-making culture of the Maori and was as specifically ritualised as wood and bone carving. The facial moko, chiselled into the skin, was as distinctive as a signature; indeed, at the time of the signing of the Treaty of Waitangi, many chiefs recorded their moko alongside their mark, where it stood both as a commitment and a statement of the existence of another culture.

For reasons that have never been precisely established, the facial moko among Maori men died out and in 1921 the historian James Cowan was unable to find anyone who had had a facial moko applied after 1865.

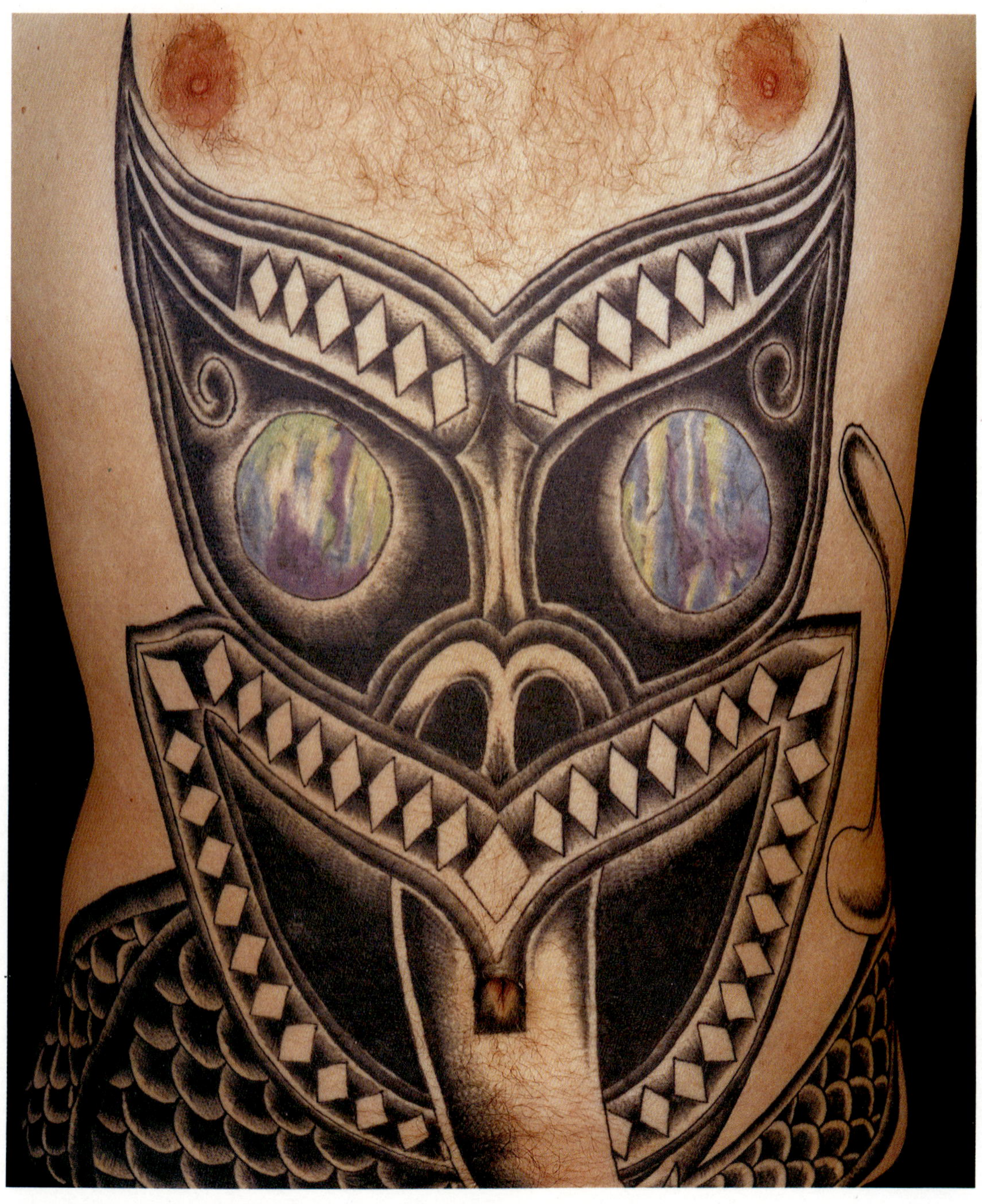

13 New Zealand Tattoo

Michael King's book, *Moko — Maori Tattooing in the 20th Century* discusses only tattoo among women, and talks of it as a practice that is dying, an entirely reasonable assumption in 1972. But recently, just as Maori culture itself has been resurgent, moko has returned, among both Maori men and women. These recent moko are not chiselled as was the ancient custom, but made with needles. Seen on a busy urban street in bright sunlight, their effect is startling. Also returning is the traditional rāpe or spiral-on-

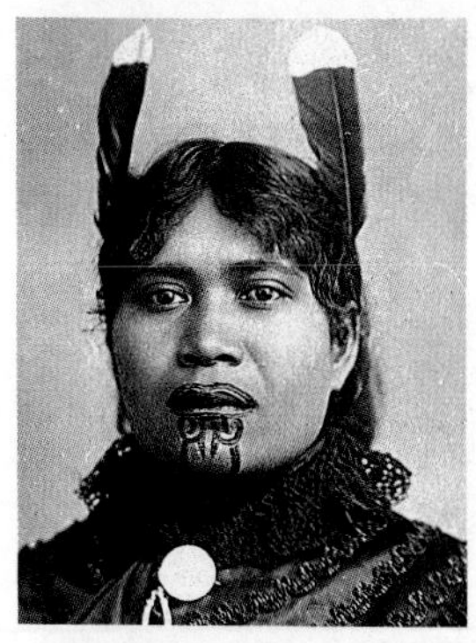

plate 6

buttocks pattern. And everywhere, braided round biceps, laced around calves, kowhaiwhai, koru and other traditional patterns can be seen.

As the Maori influence is resurgent, so the pakeha tradition is increased. While the two lines, and the separate Samoan line, maintain and develop their purity, a mingling, an absorption of influences is also taking place. By drawing on New Zealand's unique heritage, the best tattooists in this country are on their way to creating some of the most distinctive and exciting work in the world.

Nigel Cox

14 January 1994

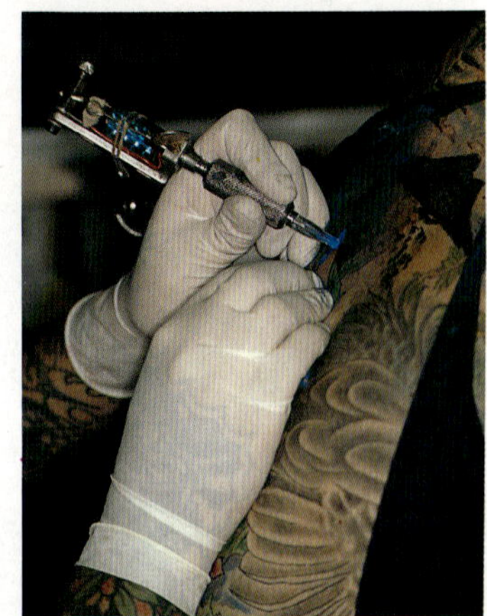

*plate 7*

*plate 1*
*Purple Humming Bird. The bird is a*
*typical choice of women, seen as*
*'feminine', and the shoulder is the usual*
*site, followed by buttocks and breasts.*
*Jude, tattooist, Palmerston North.*

*plate 2*
*European ethnologists and artists were*
*fascinated by the Polynesian tattoo. The*
*German Carl Marquardt recorded*
*Samoan styles in his* Die Tatowirung
Beider Geschlechter in Samoa *in*
*1899.*
*Auckland Institute and Museum*

*plate 3*
*Steve and Carl: heavily tattooed and*
*competing hard at the Magog Show, New*
*Plymouth. Chris Bezencon, tattooist,*
*Auckland.*

*plate 4*
*The traditional Samoan Tatu by Paulo*
*Sulu'ape, generally regarded as the best*
*known Samoan Tattoo Artist in New*
*Zealand.*

*plate 5*
*Although Maori men ceased having the*
*moko applied in the mid-nineteenth*
*century, the practice continued on a*
*reduced scale among Maori women,*
*despite the efforts of the church to*
*discourage it.*
*Alexander Turnbull Library*

*plate 6*
*Detail of 'Arai Te Uru', the taniwha*
*tattooed on Glenn, shown on page 37.*
*Phil Matthias, tattooist, Auckland.*

*plate 7*
*Graham Cavanagh, Auckland tattooist, at*
*work.*

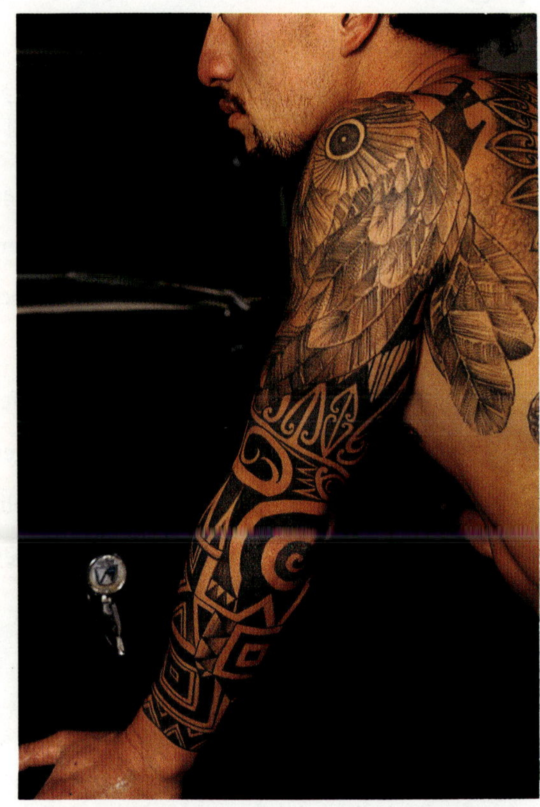

then, turning on the machine, explained briefly how it worked. He did a couple of small strokes on the skin, stopped and asked if that felt OK.

I was impressed. Here was a man who must have done thousands of tattoos, yet takes the time to make sure his client is comfortable. He is a modest man who loves his work. When asked what he does in his spare time, he answered, 'I draw tattoo designs.' Obviously the key to success is commitment.

Roger Ingerton works in Wellington.

Craig, Family Owl, Whangarei, from his
Mother's side.

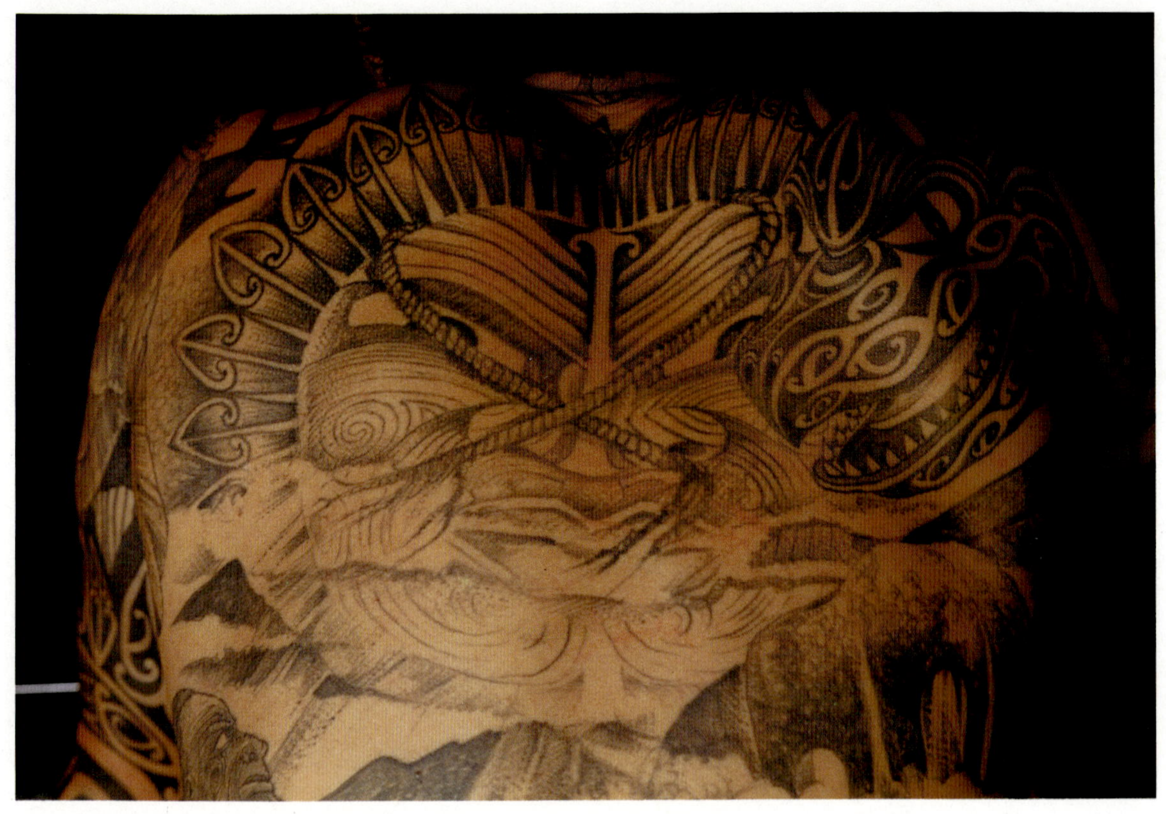

Craig: back depicts the sun being caught by
Maui and Taniwha.

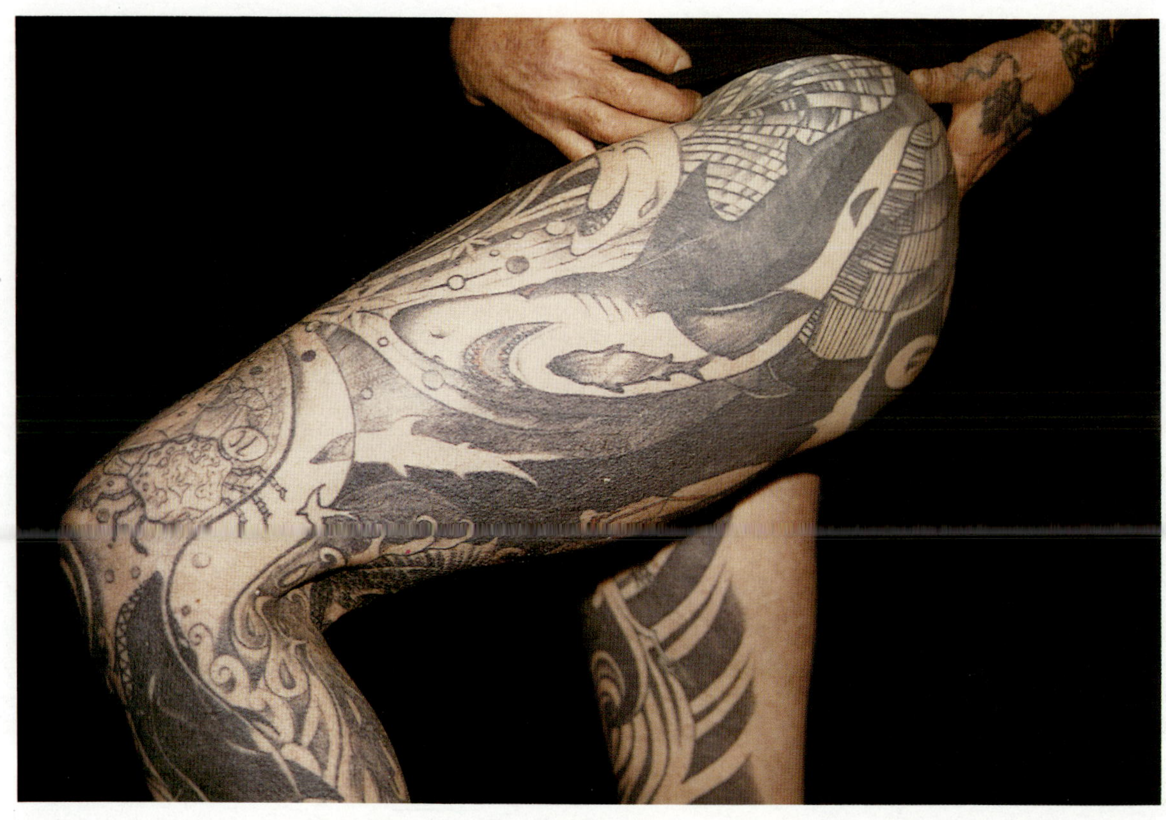

Roger: self-tattooed legs.

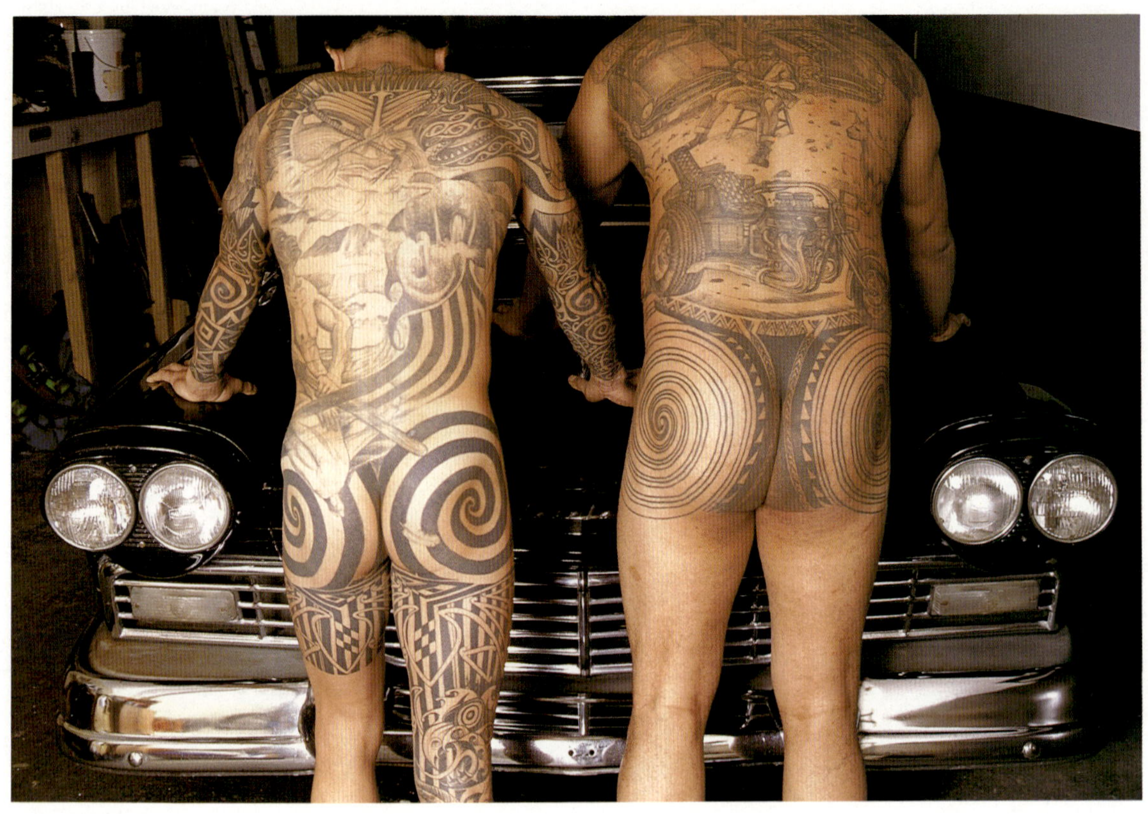

Craig and Mike with their 1958 Ford Fairlane.

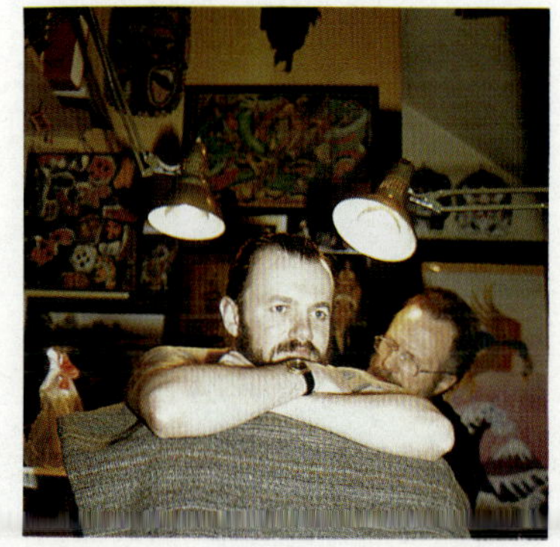

Roger at work.

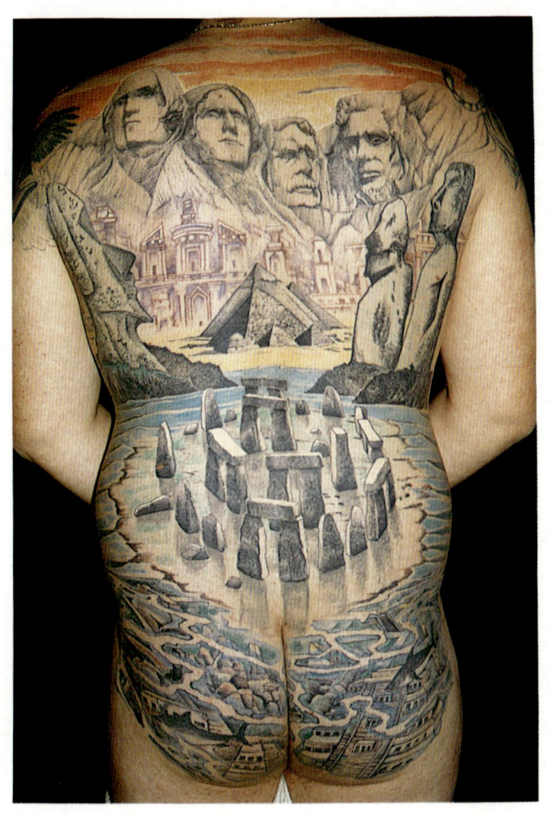 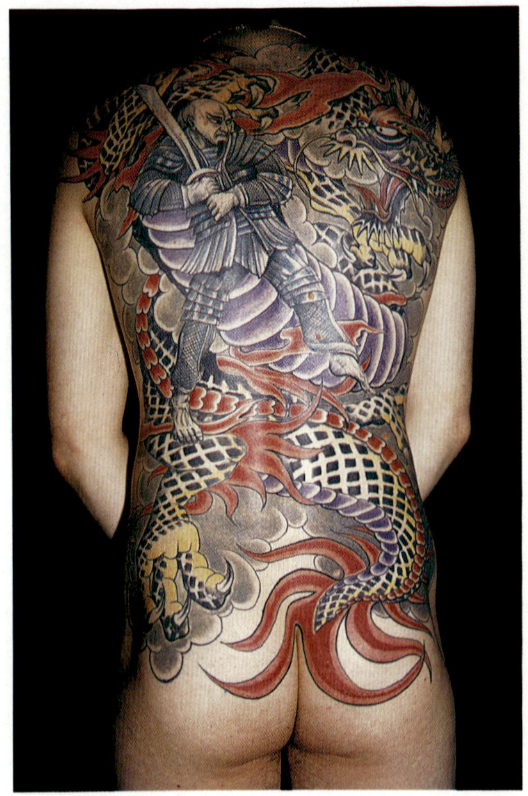

Howard, editor of *The Heavily Tattooed Club* magazine.

Ian, manufacturing jeweller.

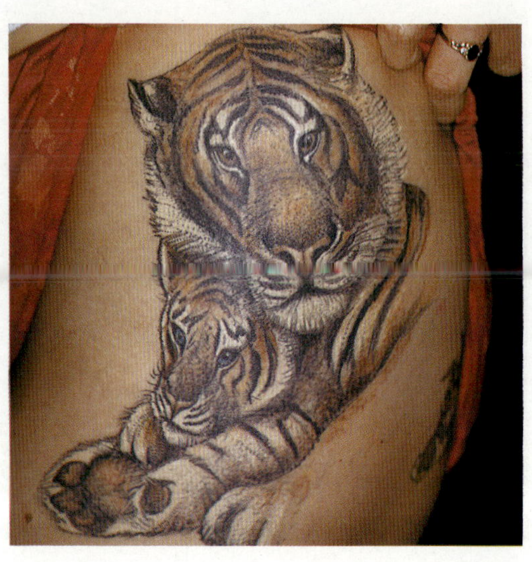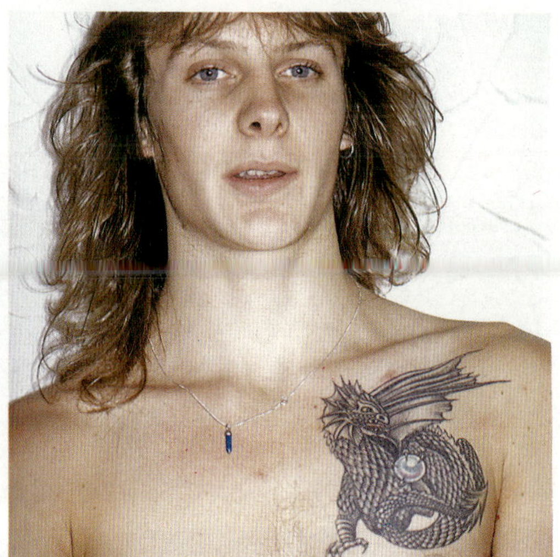

Connie. Loves big cats.

Leith: dragon holding ball of wisdom.

Mark, bookstore manager.

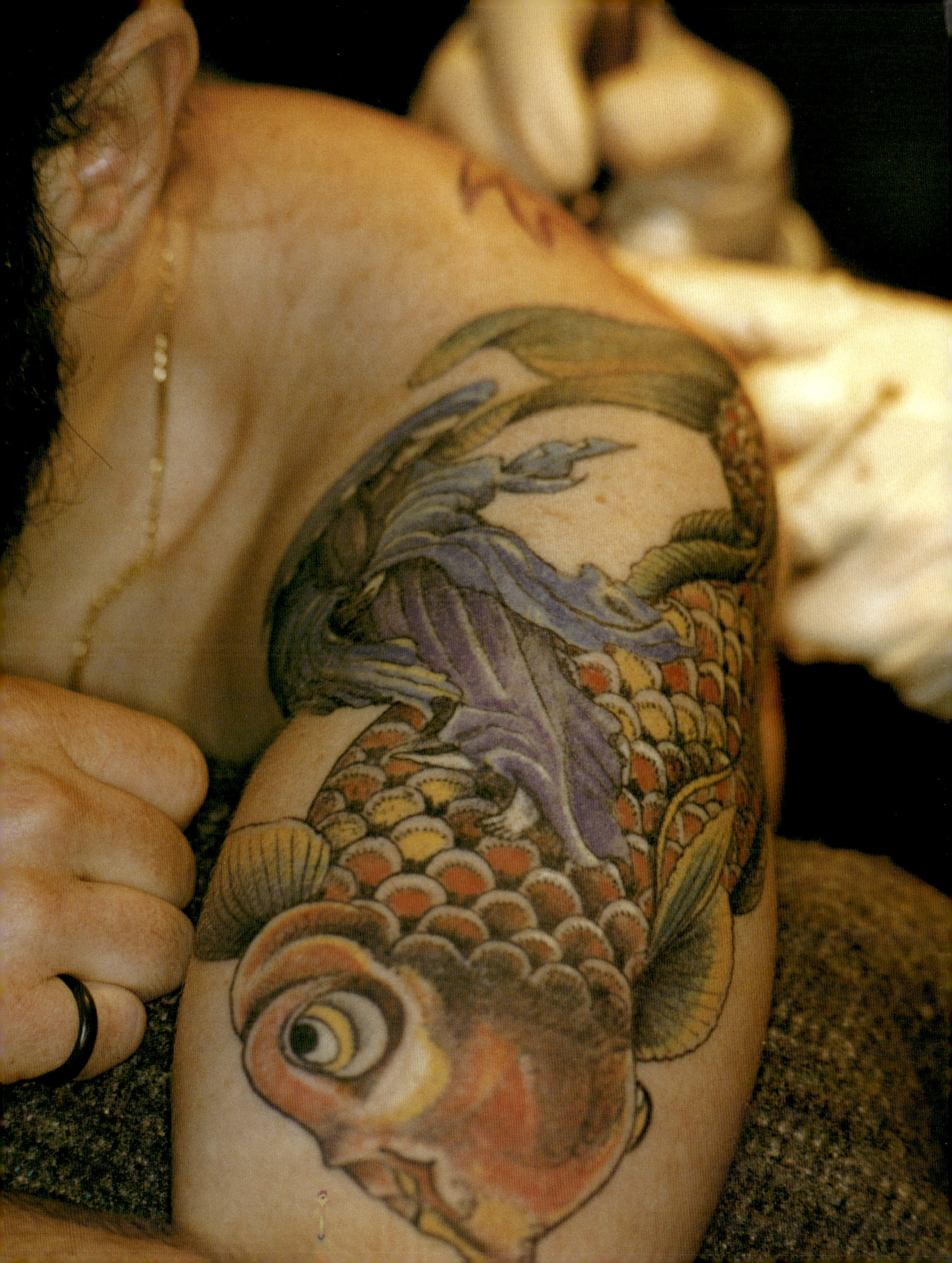

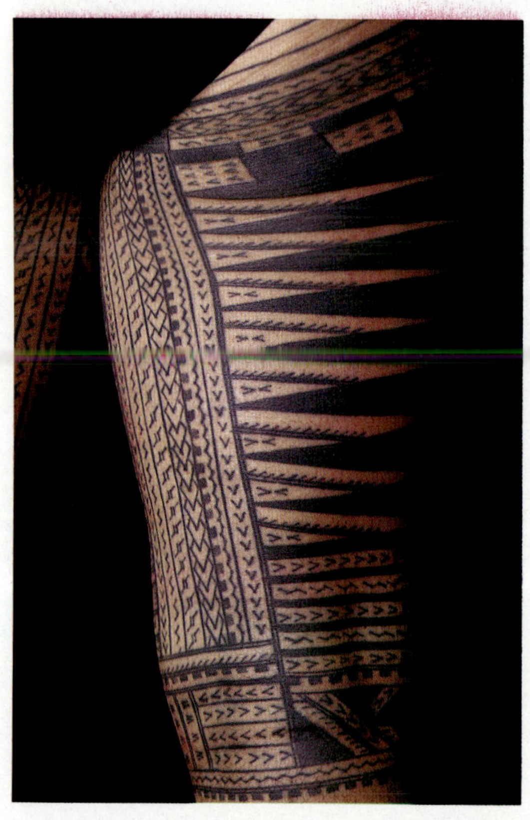

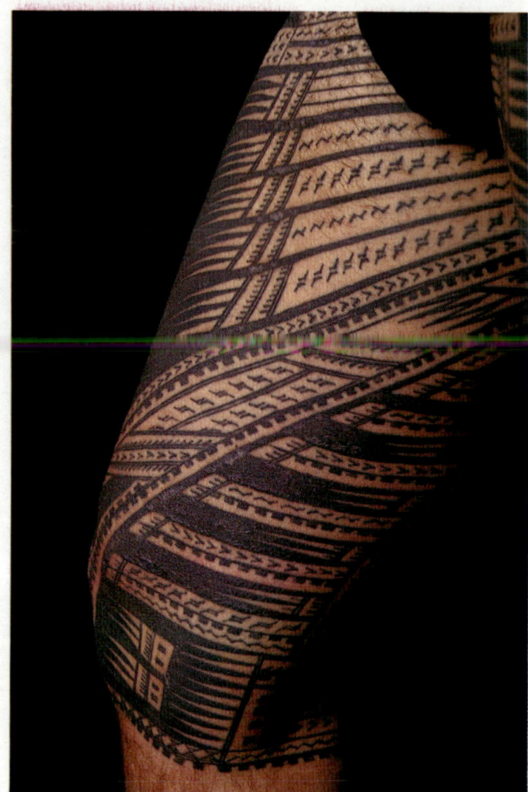

Kevin, police constable, 5th Dan black belt
karate. Legs tattooed in three sittings.


Mike, tattoo artist.

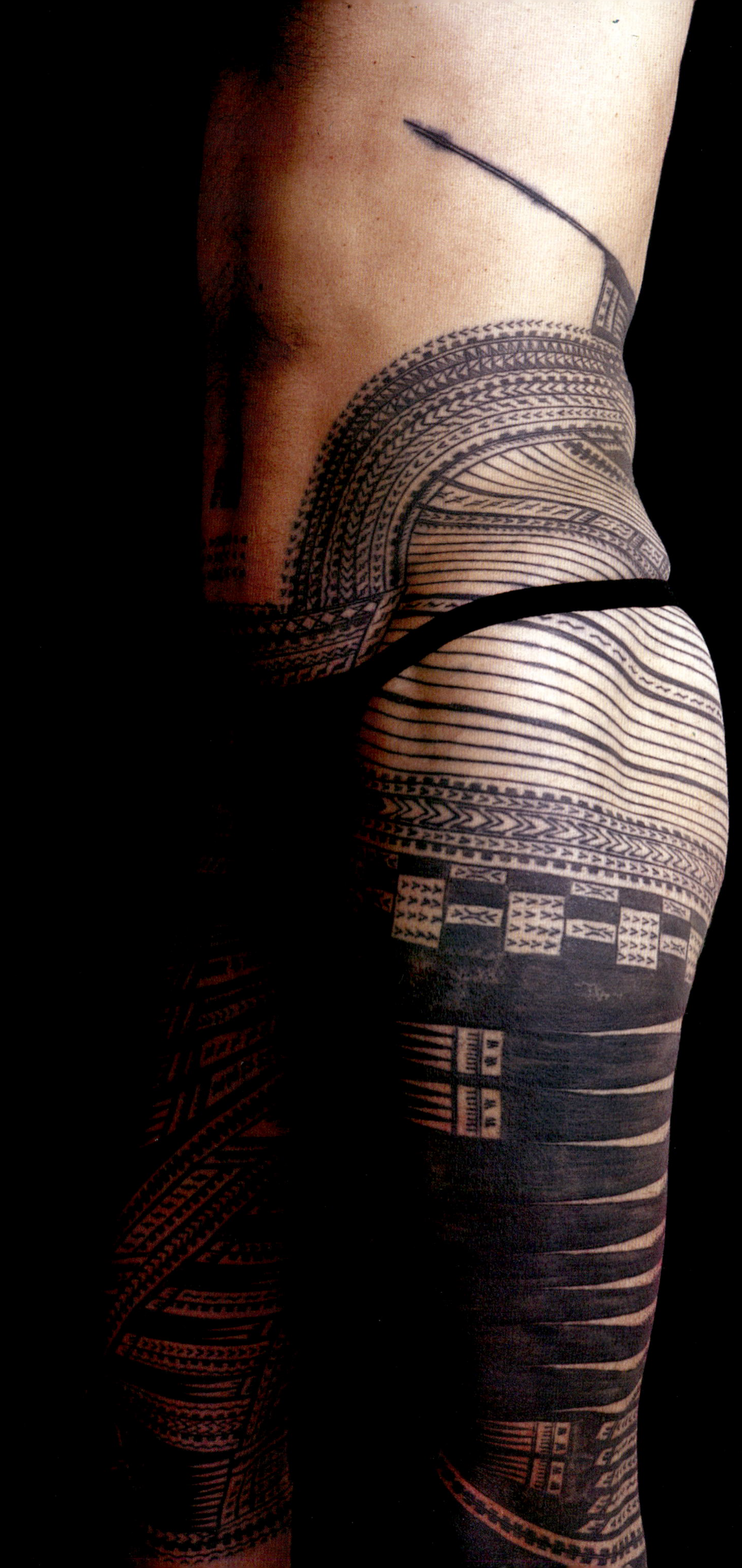

Mike, tattoo artist.

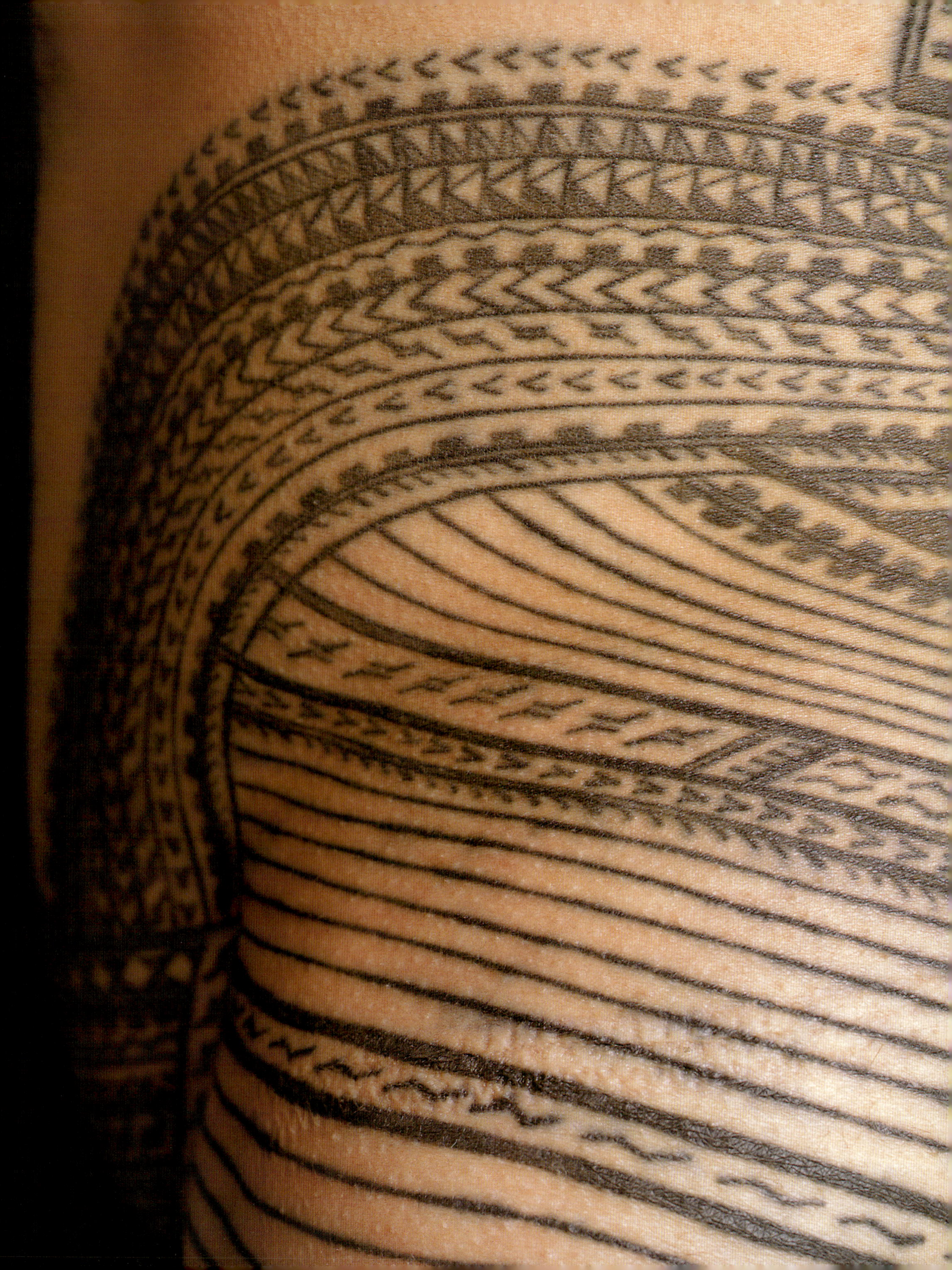

# R O N   M A H O N

A REAL KIWI BLOKE, hard-case, opinionated and humorous, Ron loves tattooing. He works from home, and is a real family man. Donna helps him by drawing designs and keeps him on the straight and narrow. He talks a lot while working, which appears to relax his clients.

Situated on the shore of the Waikato river, opposite the power station with huge chimneys dominating the skyline, the little studio where people bare their skin to the needle and ink is obviously a well-known local haunt — people driving past sound their horns and wave.

Ron Mahon works in Huntly.

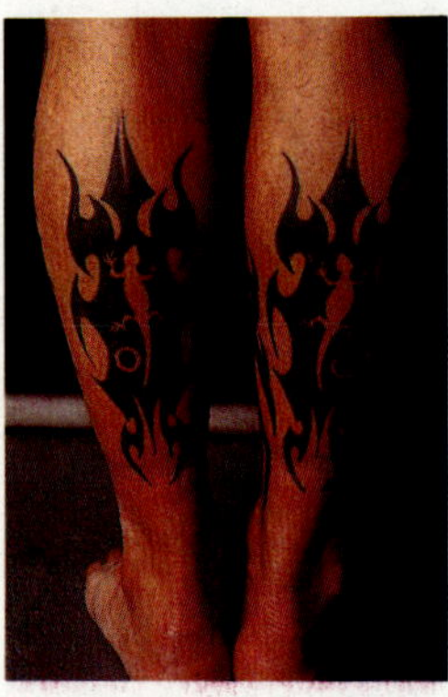

Selwyn, driver. Tuatara design, within tribal
tattoos.

Donna, married to Ron. Award-winning tattoo
which reflects her New Zealand heritage.

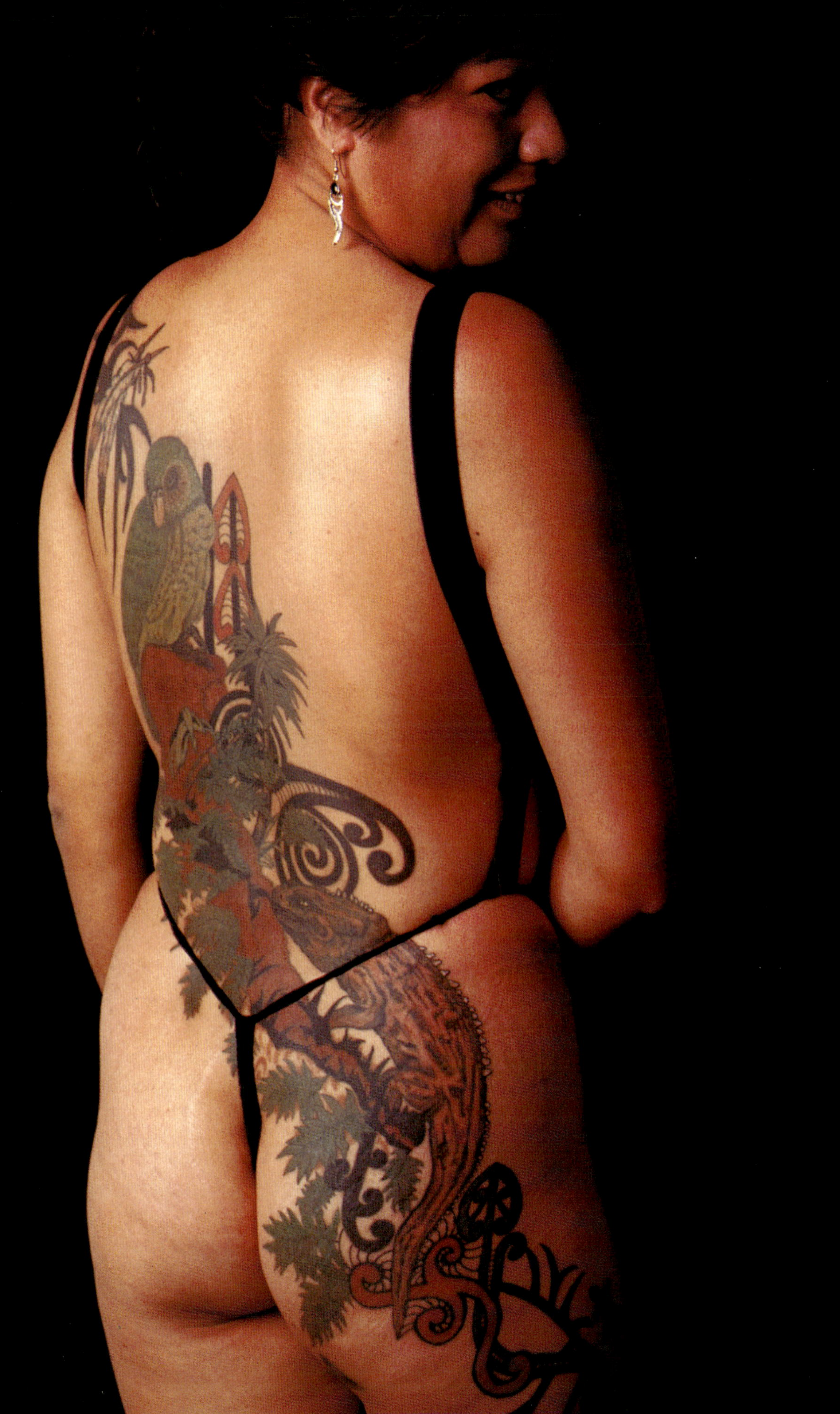

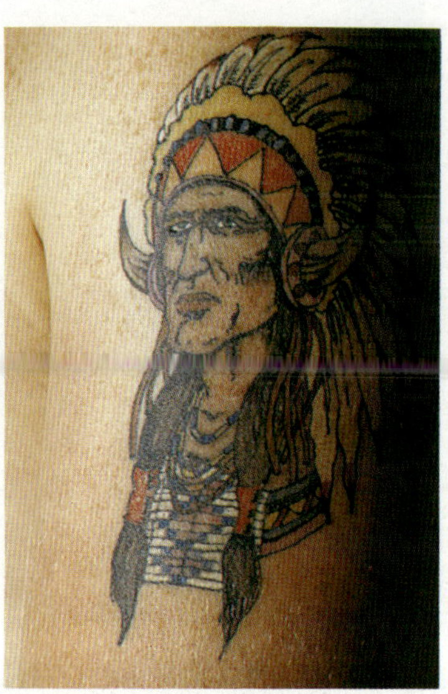 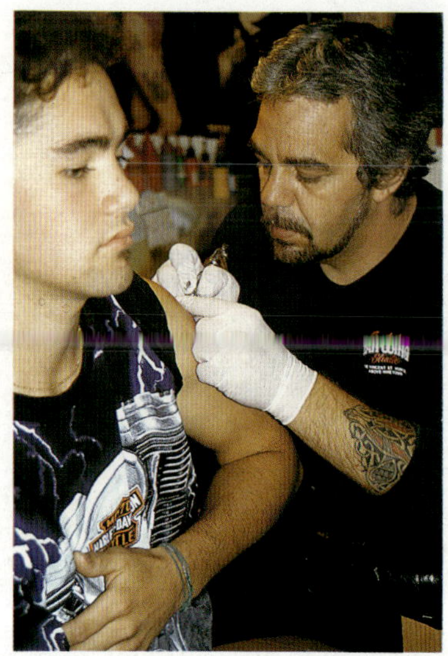

Brent: interested in the American Indian.

Ron Mahon at work.

Kevin in uniform. Work by Ron Mahon and
Eagle Neil.

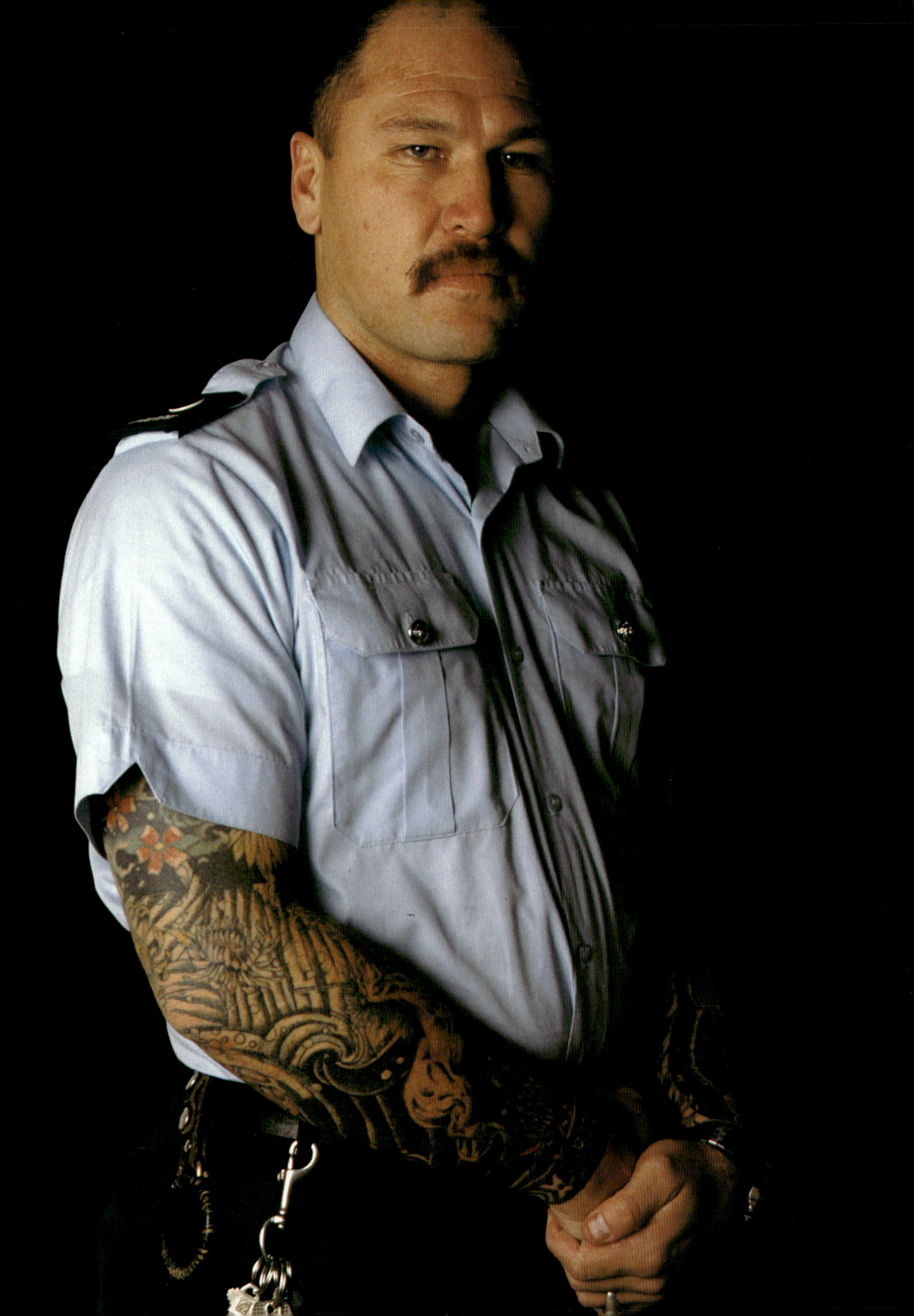

'PHIL OF COLLEGE HILL' runs a very prominent tattoo studio, trendy and colourful with a sign that says, 'Little pricks make a lasting impression'.

It took some time for Phil to take me seriously as a photographer. He doesn't suffer fools. In the past photographers had sought his cooperation and then failed to deliver the goods. However, I seemed to convince him I was serious and he directed me to some of his clients with wonderful tattoos.

Phil Matthias works in Auckland.

Glenn, builder.

This piece is called 'Arai Te Uru', the name of the Sea God who protected the canoe *Takitimu* in which Glenn's father's people journeyed from Rarotonga to Aotearoa. The actual tattoo design came from his father's *Tokotoko* (talking stick) and is one of five Taniwha. The tattoo was started 21st November 1992, and was completed after 20 hour's work, on 16th April 1992.

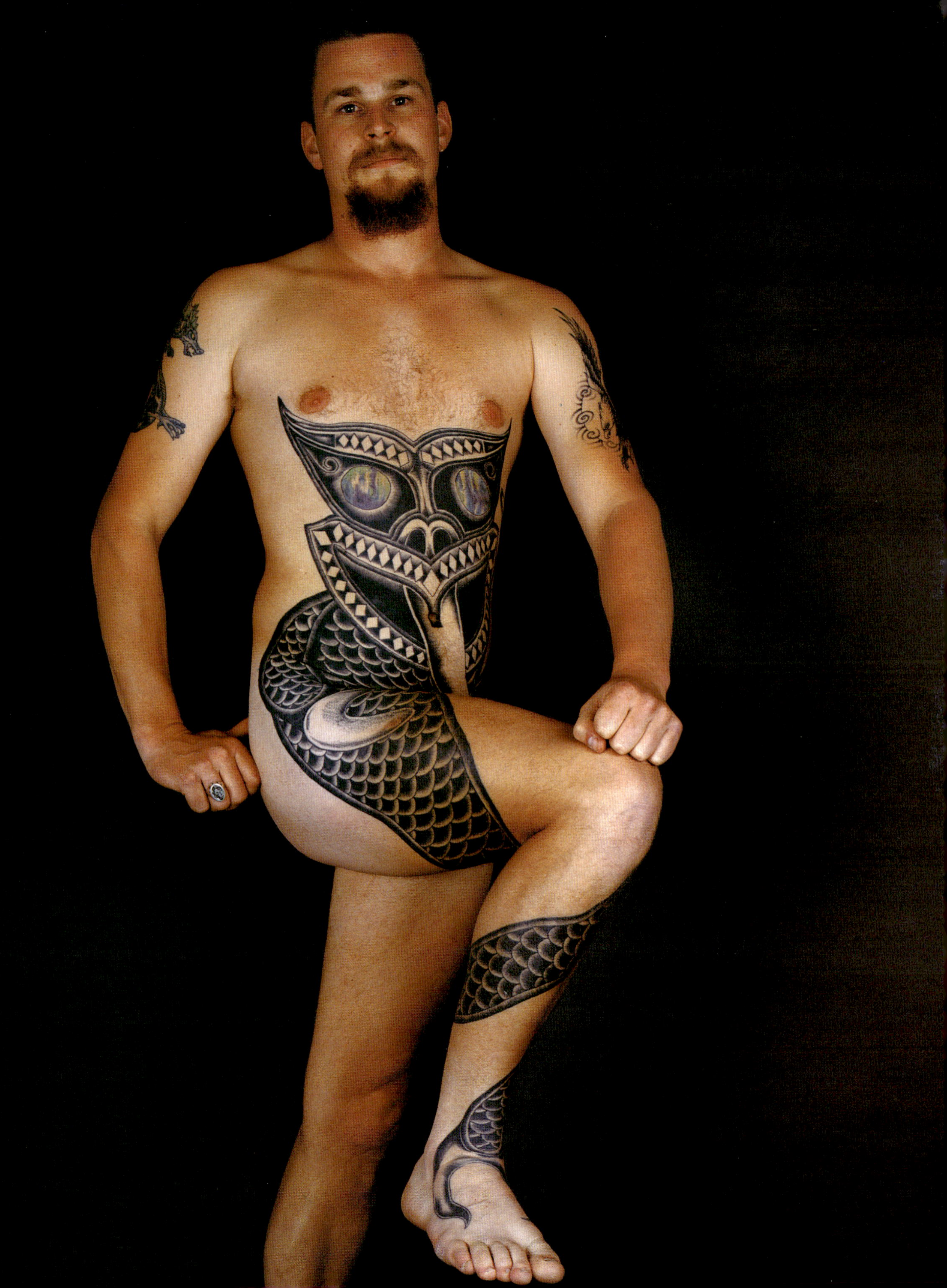

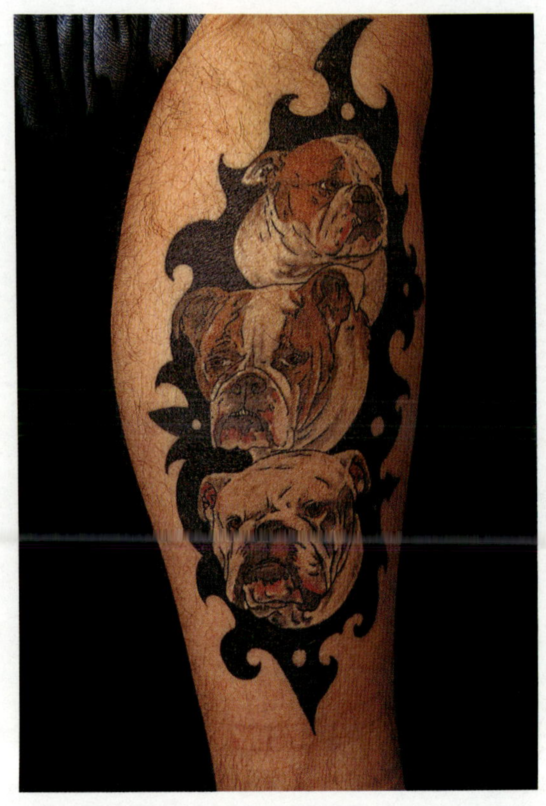

Neil, pet shop manager. Portraits of his bulldogs. Top: Bonzo, middle: Zoe, bottom: Saxon (friend's dog).

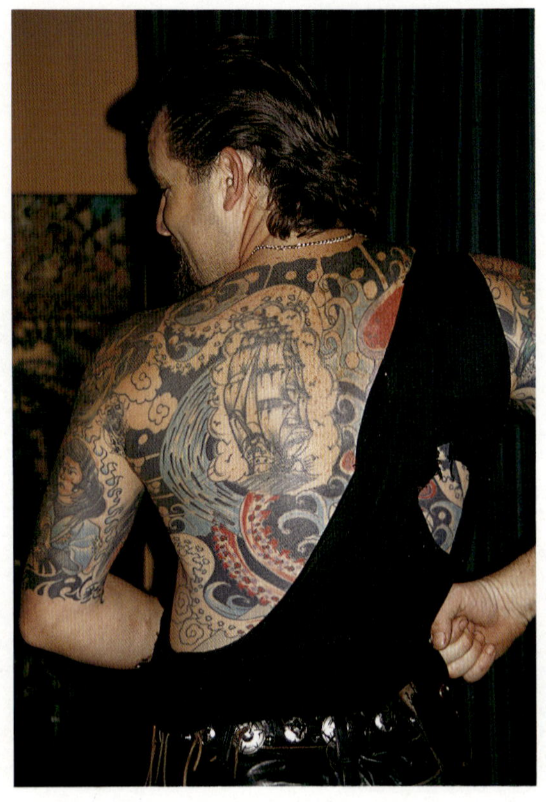

Mark, Harley enthusiast.

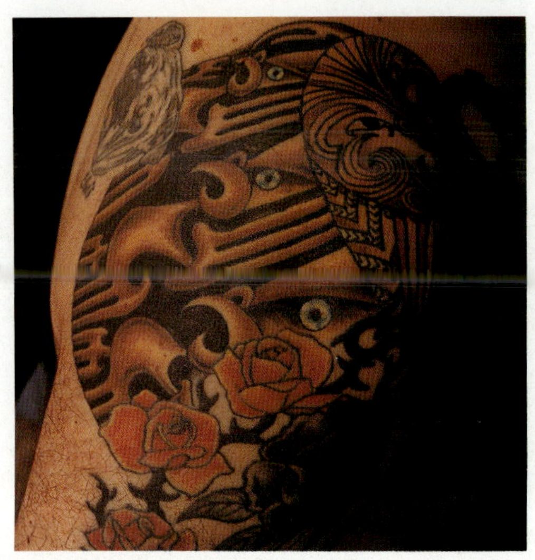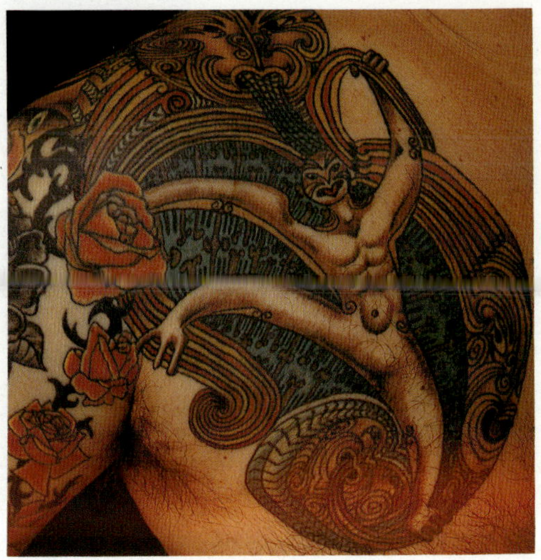

Kerry, music store assistant. His design reflects
his Maori heritage.

Jo Cool: detail at right.

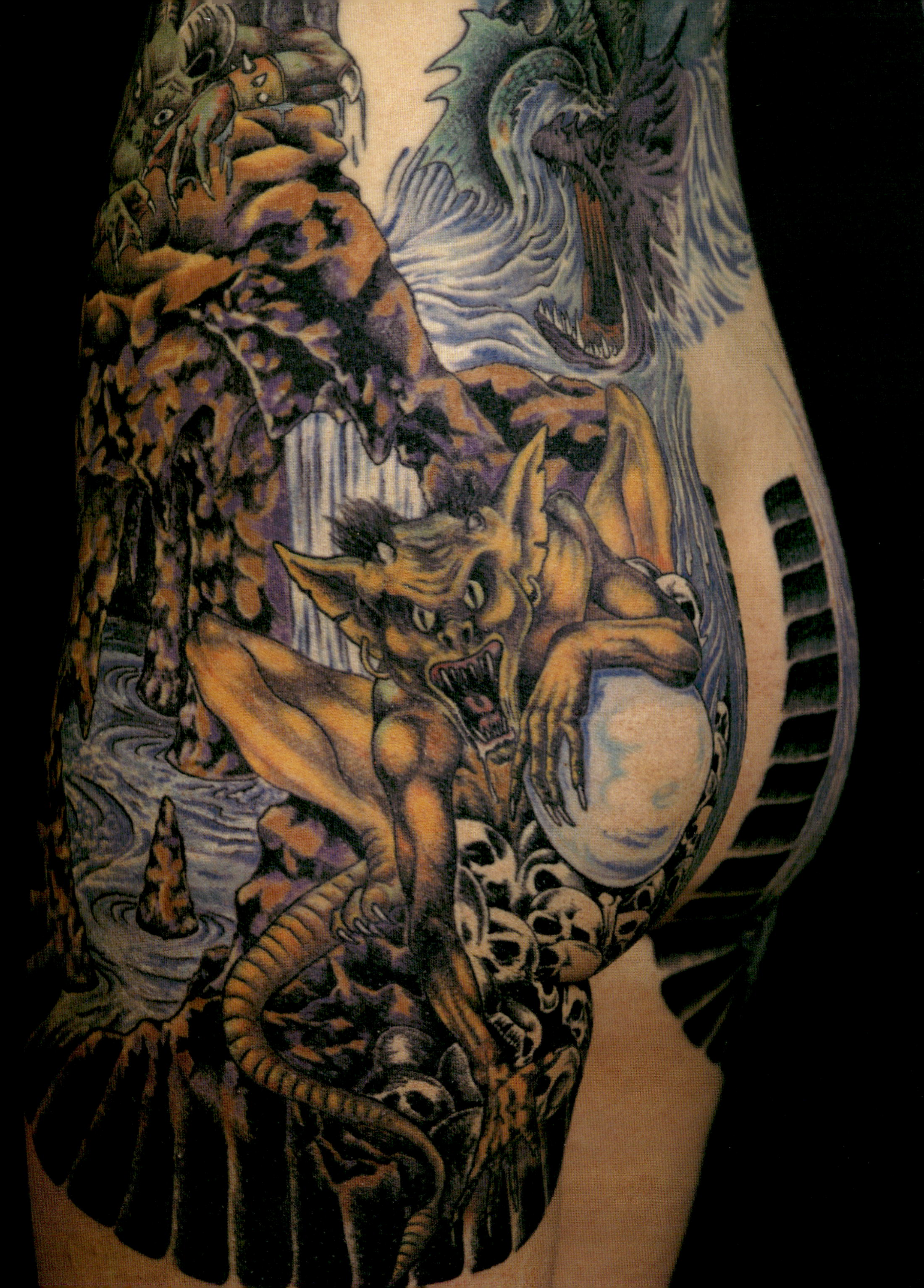

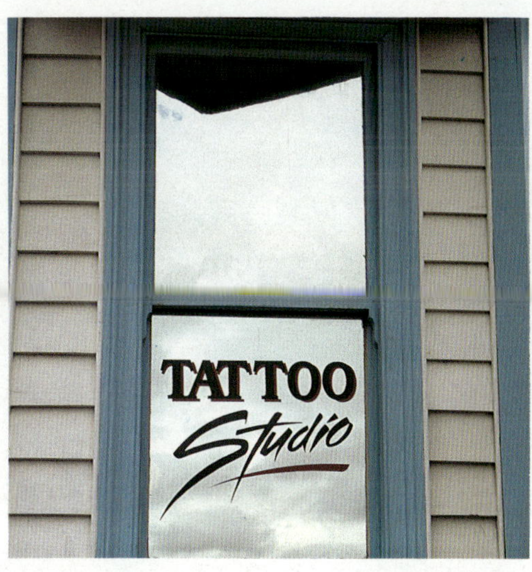


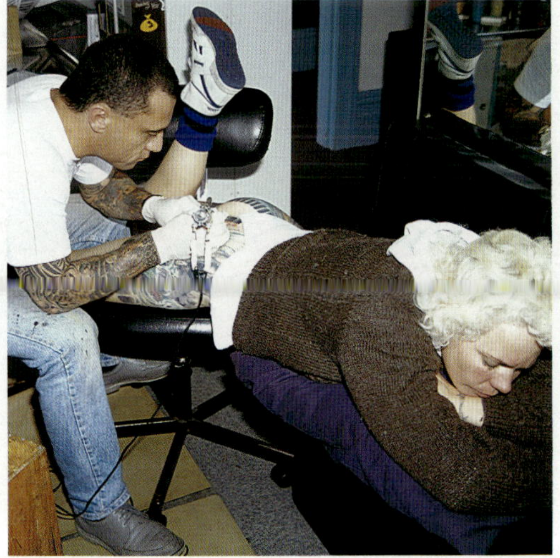

Phil's studio in Ponsonby and Phil working on
Jo.

Jo Cool, at right.

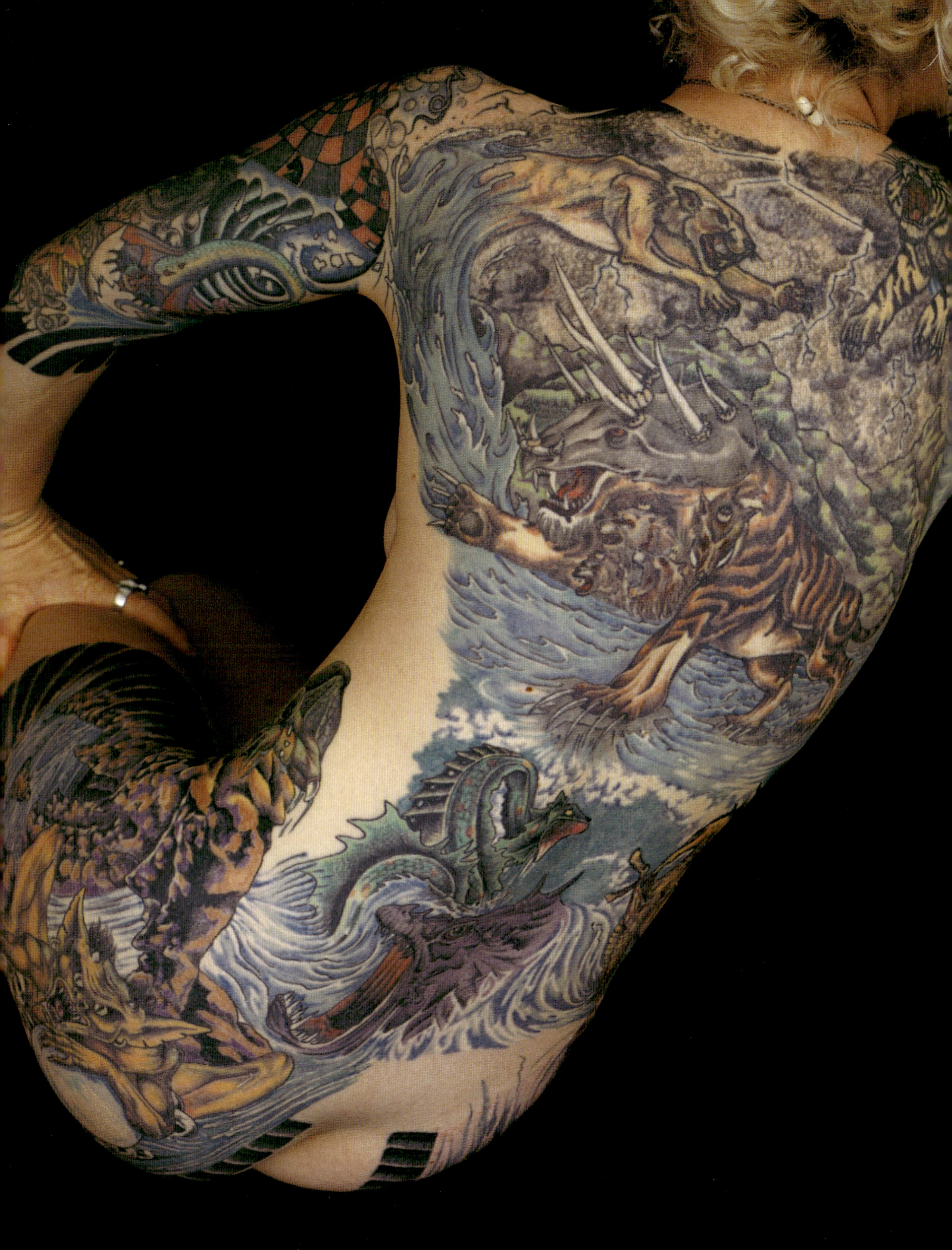

STU HAS COME TO TATTOOING from a background in graphic art. He worked in the printing industry before taking the plunge and opening his own studio.

Introspective and discerning, Stu expresses himself in the finely detailed and intensely coloured designs he executes. In a short time he has built up a loyal following of satisfied clients. His partner, Rose, is enthusiastic about Stu's tattoos and displays an award-winning example of his work. Stu Brewer works in Paraparaumu.

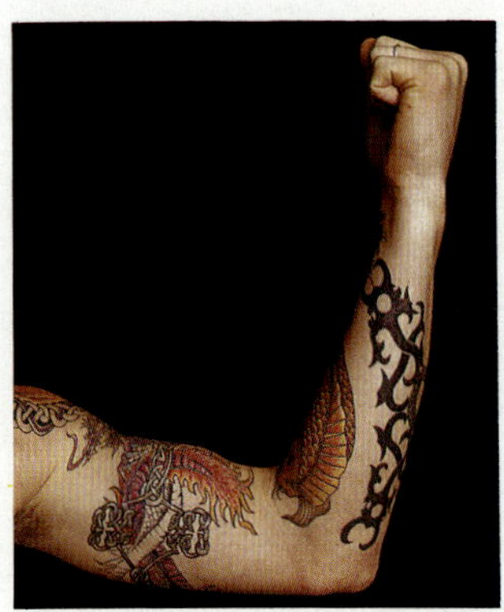

Dave D: incorporates Libra starsign with celtic design.

Tony, plasterer. Tattoos depict his family and his fascination with American Indians.

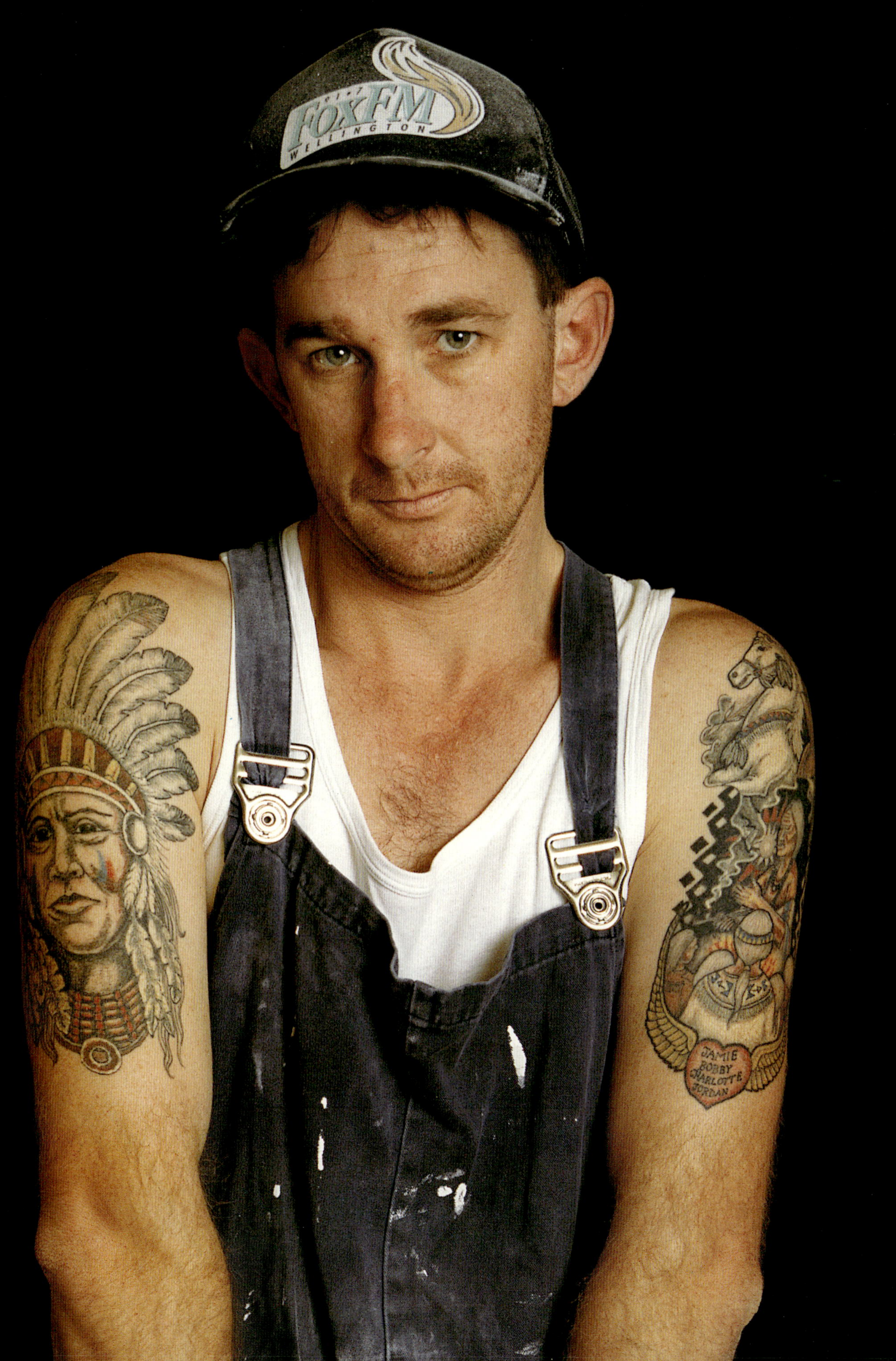

FOX FM
WELLINGTON
JAMIE
BOBBY
CHARLOTTE
JORDAN

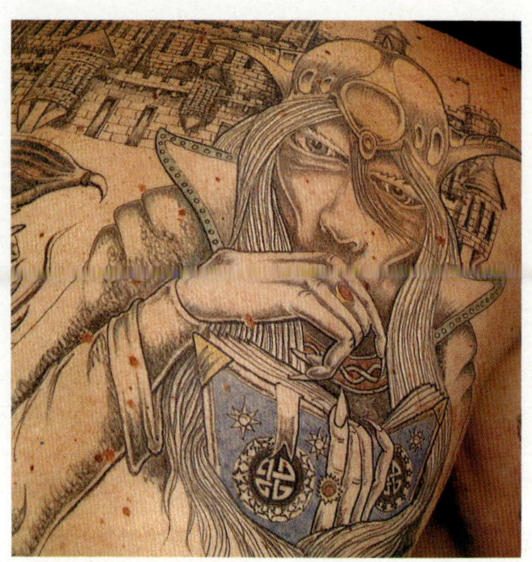 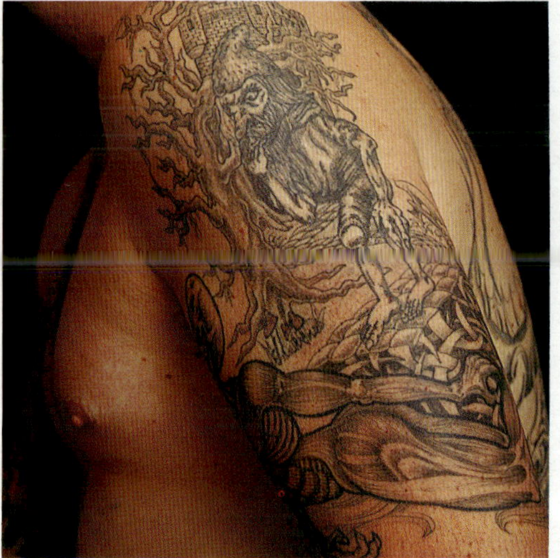

Vaughan, butcher.

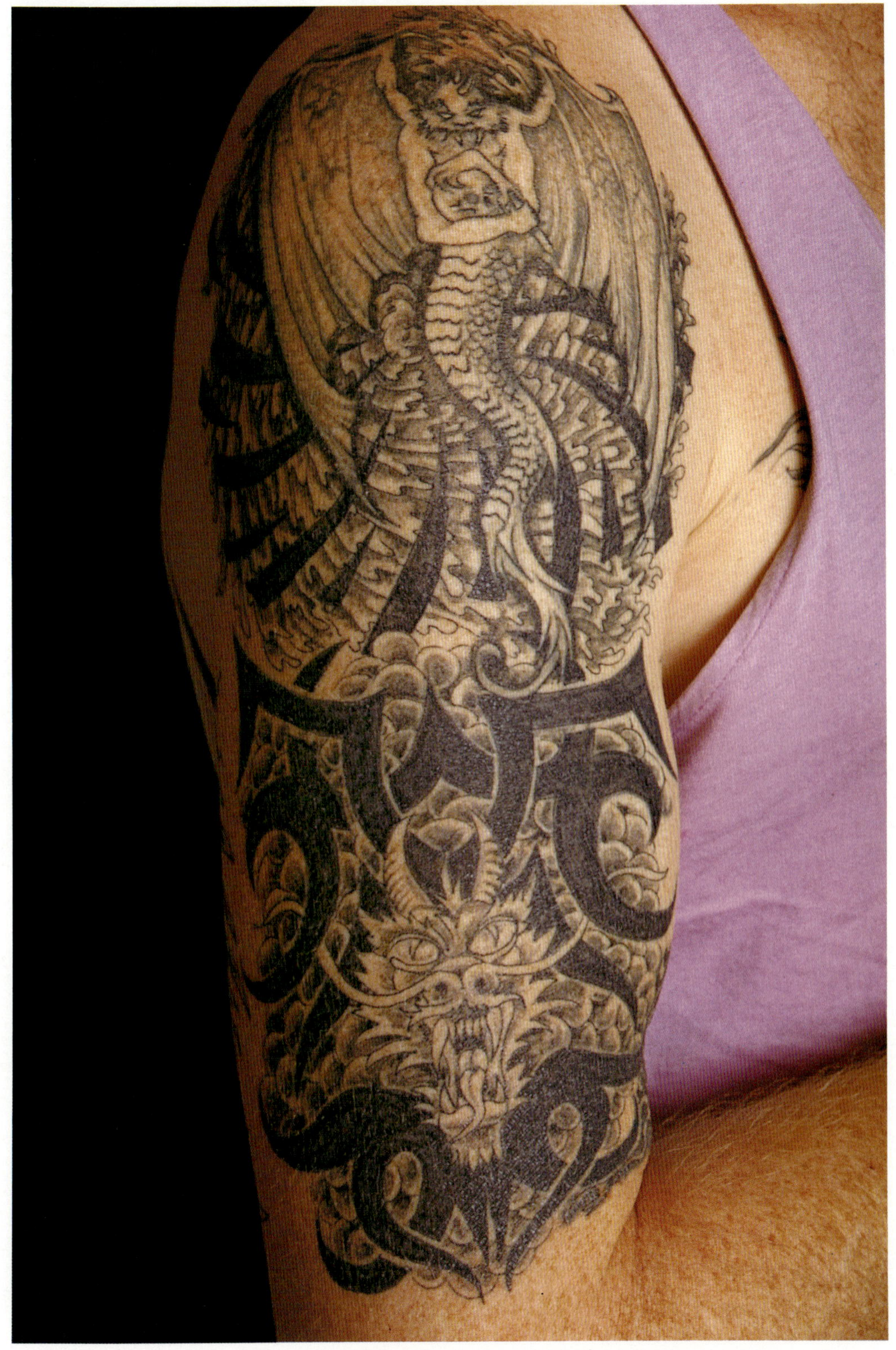

Dave S. Interested in goblins and demons.
Fantasy tattoos.

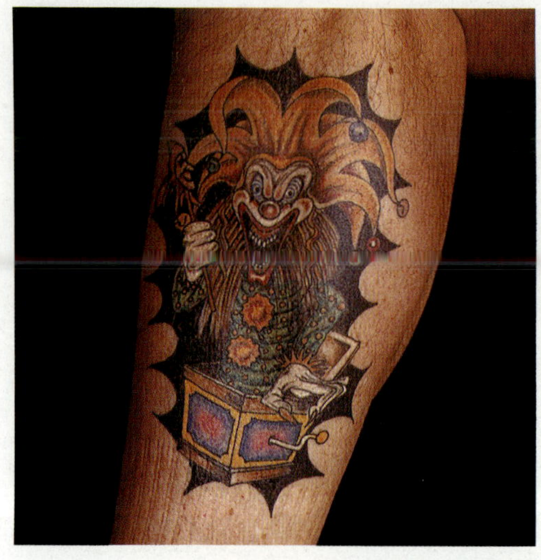

Guy, café manager. Jack-in-the-Box.

Rose, Stu and Kimberlee.

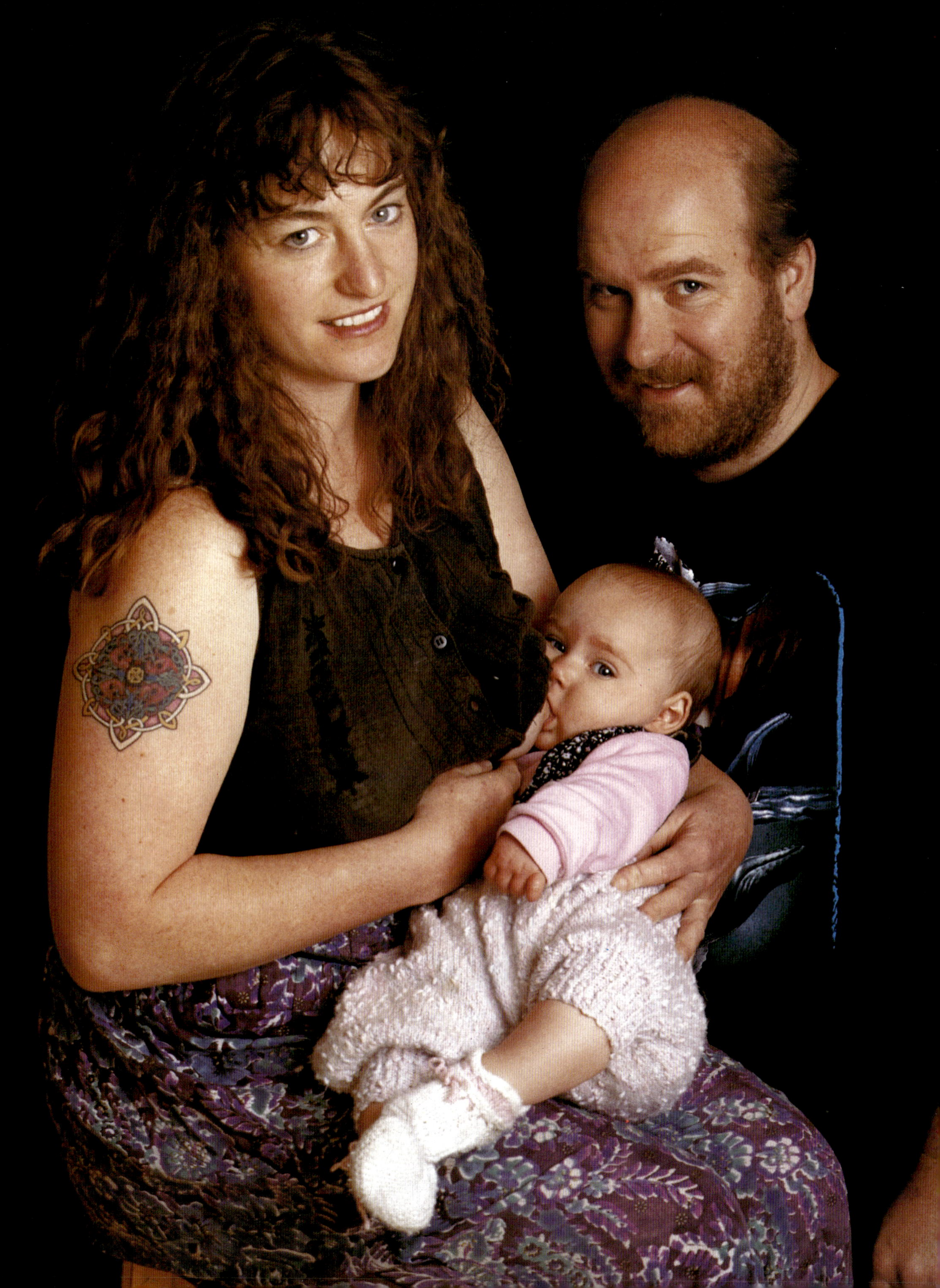

# R O B   K R A U S E

ROB IS A QUIET, DEDICATED person, serious about tattoo and giving it a good image. He is the president of TAANZ, which is trying to elevate the status of tattoo and stamp out backyarders. As Rob stresses, complying with the Health Department regulations is of prime importance for all tattooists.

It was no trouble for Rob and partner Chris to organise a group of clients to be photographed, and the photo session soon turned into a party. The star turn was their dog who has a Bart Simpson tattoo on her chest.

Rob Krause works in Auckland.

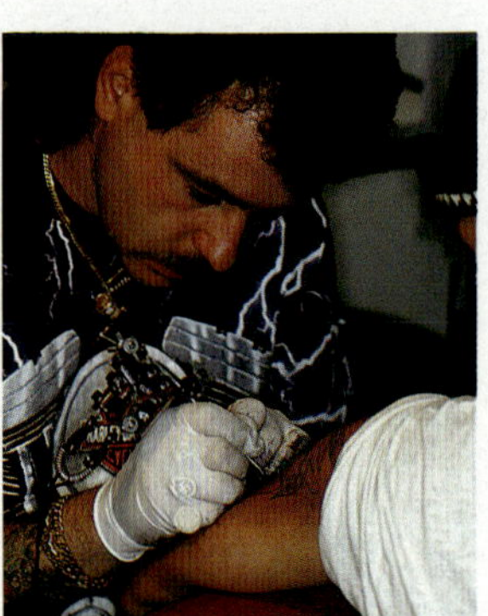

Rob working.

Wayne (Bones), groundsman.

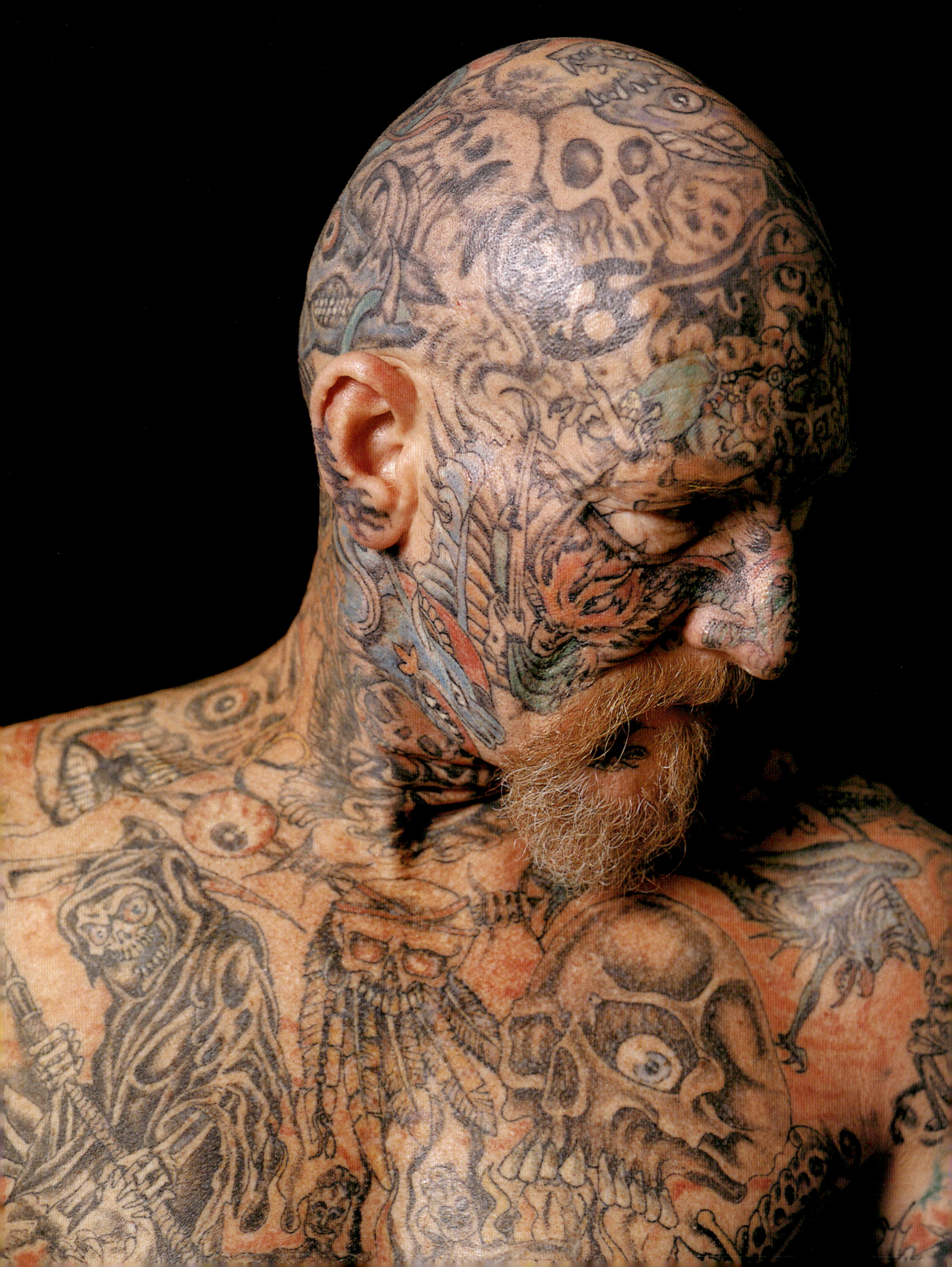

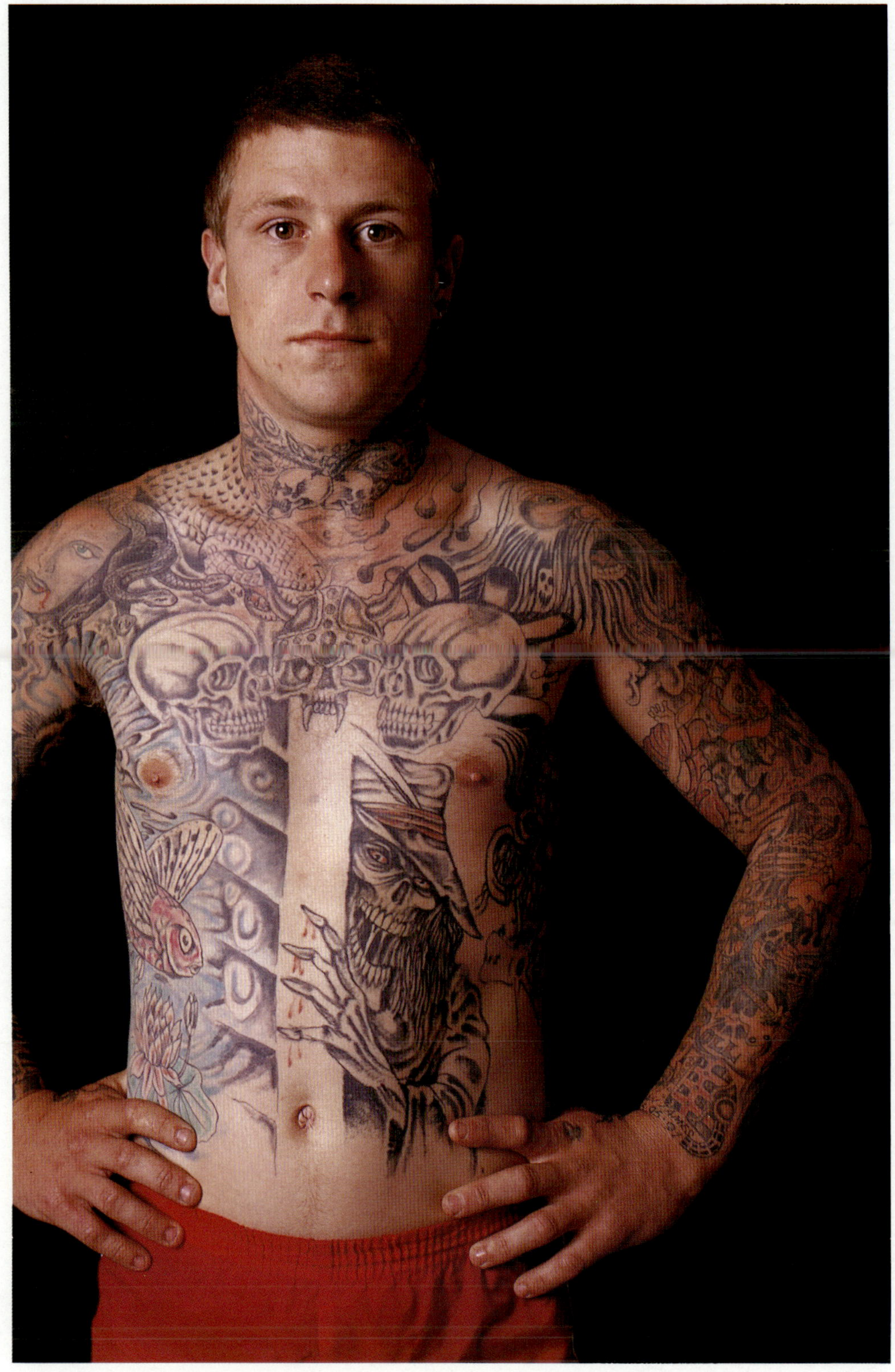

Errol.

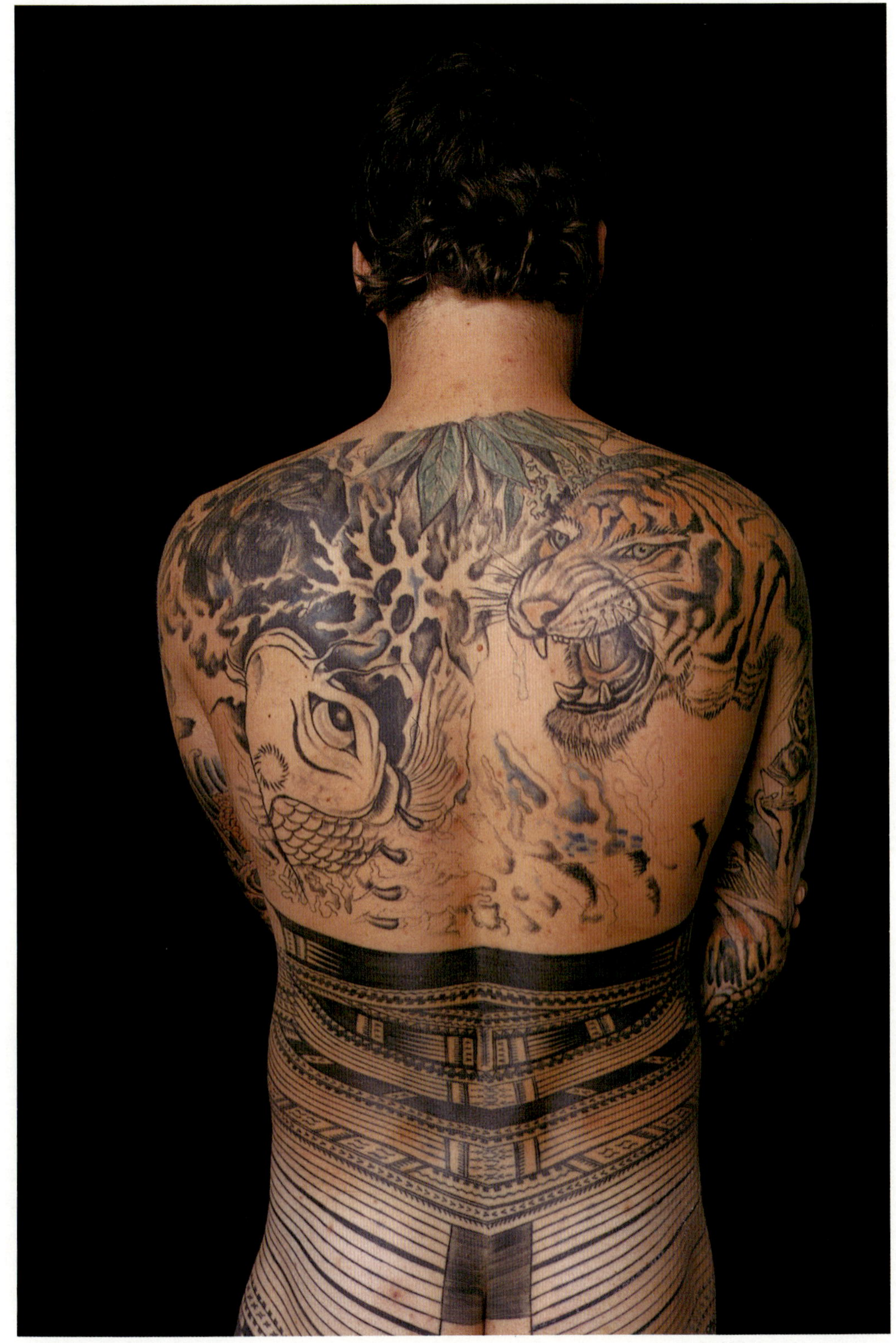

John: Conventional tattoo by Rob, *P'ea* Samoan
traditional tattoo by Paulo.

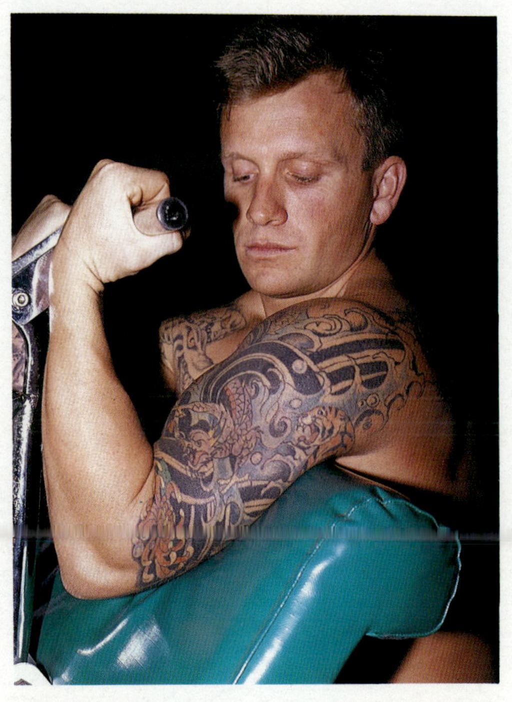

Glenn, builder.

Joce and Graham.

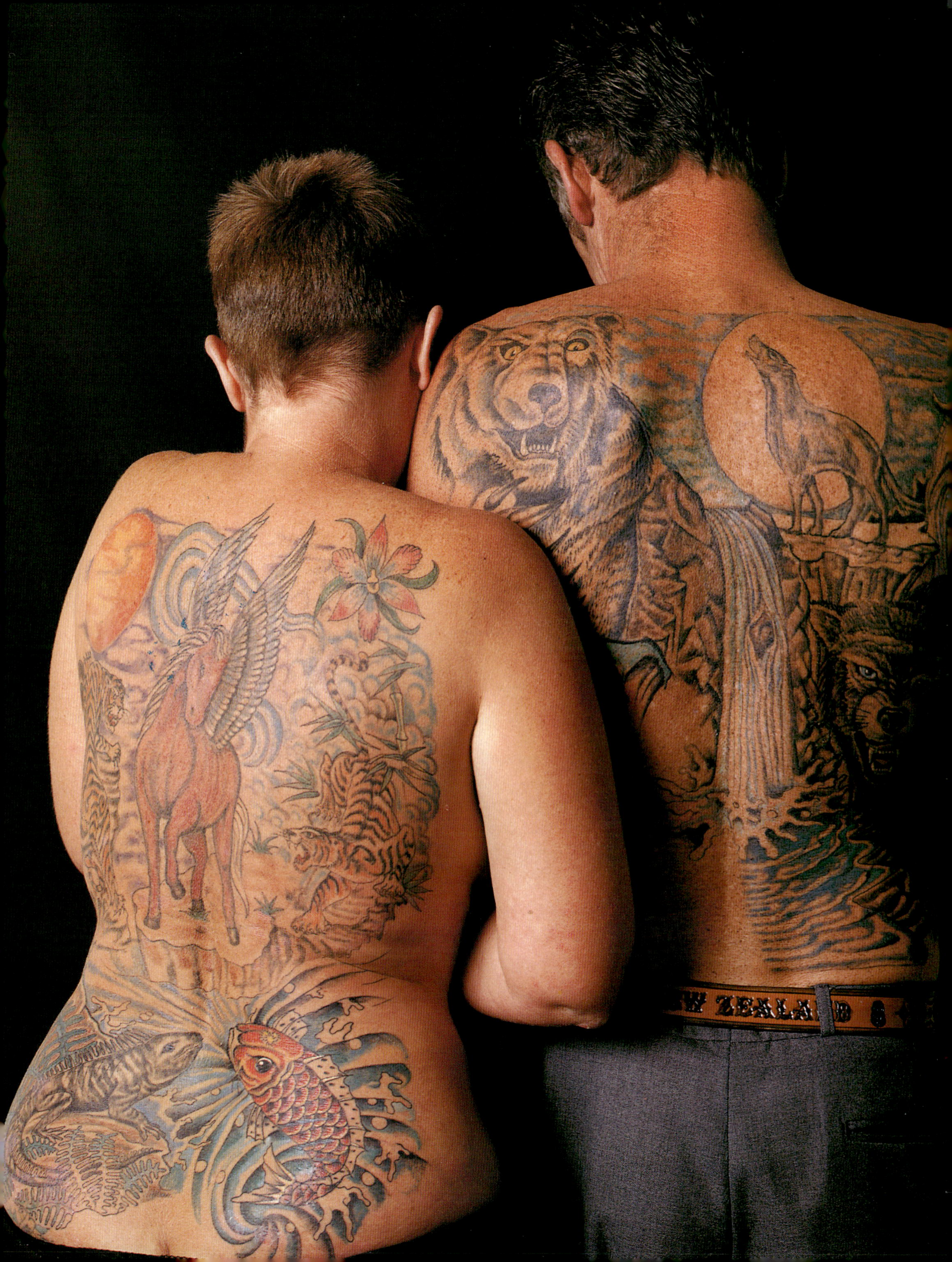
NEW ZEALAND

'DR PAIN' — A CHARACTER OF QUICK wit and dry humour.

At school his artistic style caused friction with his teachers who could not cope with a student intent on following his own design sense. Uninspired by the prospect of life as a fitter and turner, he began to pursue his interest in tattoo, and was taken under the wing of a professional to learn the art. Before long, he had his own business. Chris is serious about tattoo and to some degree has an artistic temperament. He relishes a challenge and seeks new areas for inspiration.

He is a joker and teases his clients, at times unmercifully, which appears to put them at their ease. While they are working out what he meant, they forget the pain for a moment. His place of work is a meeting place for friends and customers, who are one big family.

Chris Bezencon works in Auckland.

Jackie, printing representative and Andy, hotel manager.

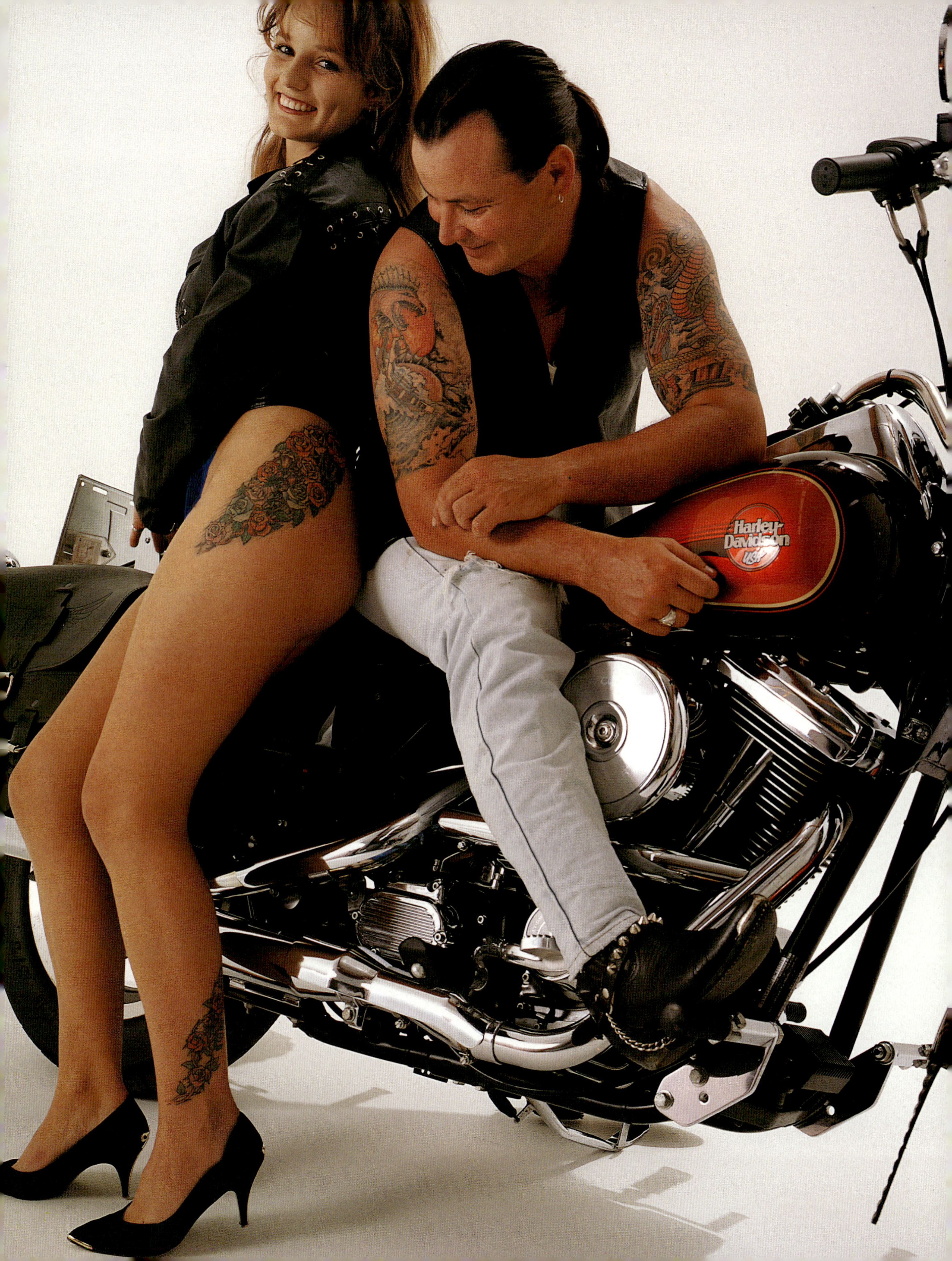
Harley
Davidson
USA

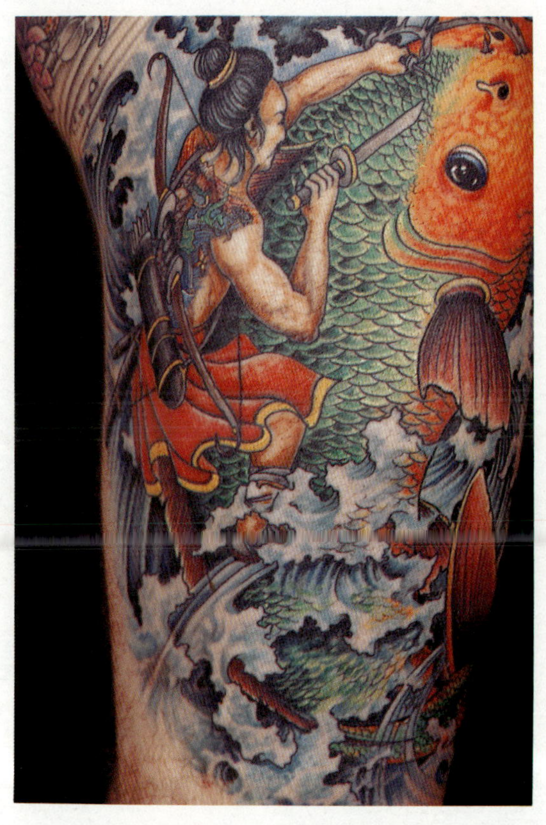

Lyall, panel-beater, and son A.J.

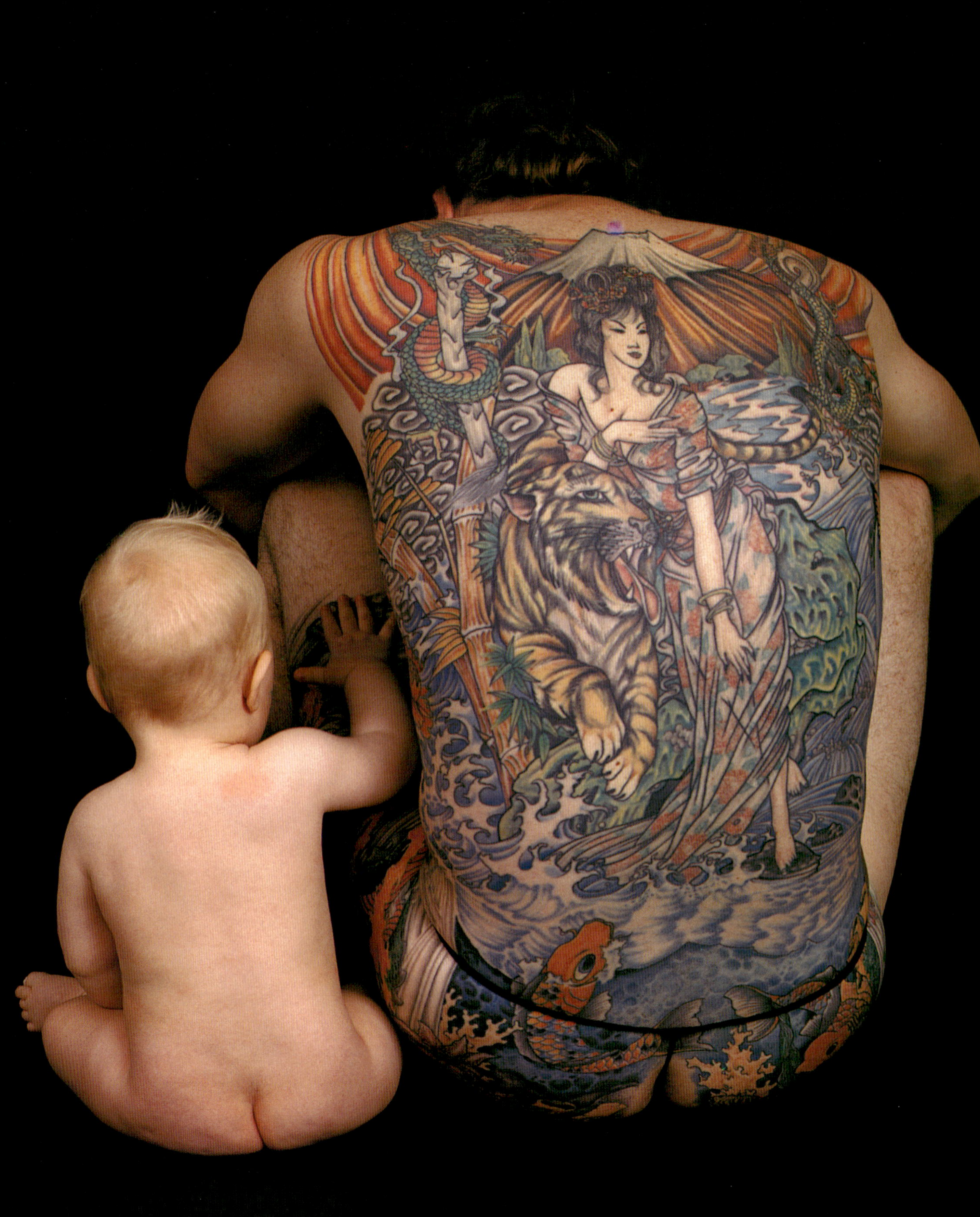

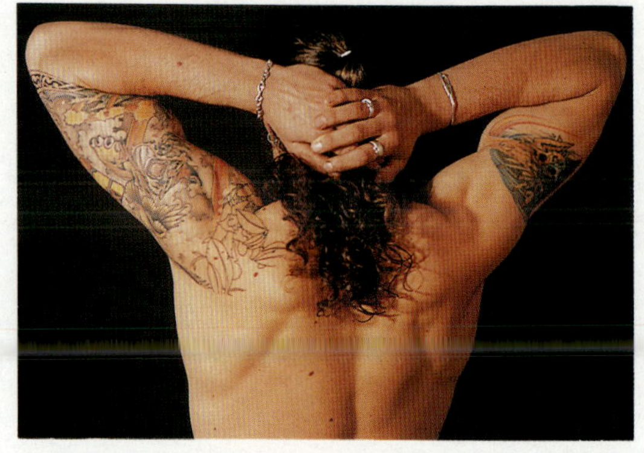

Anthony, artist.

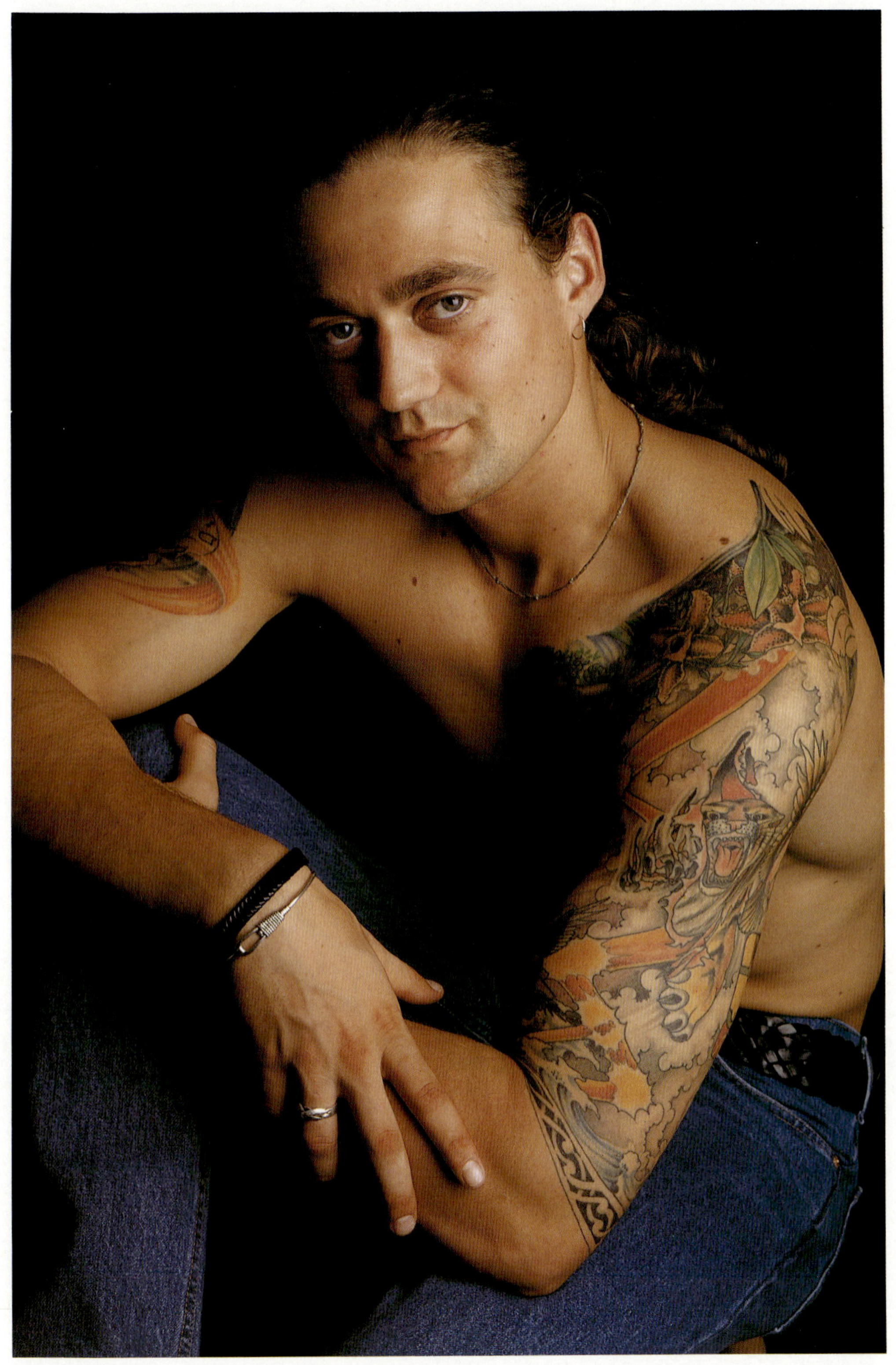

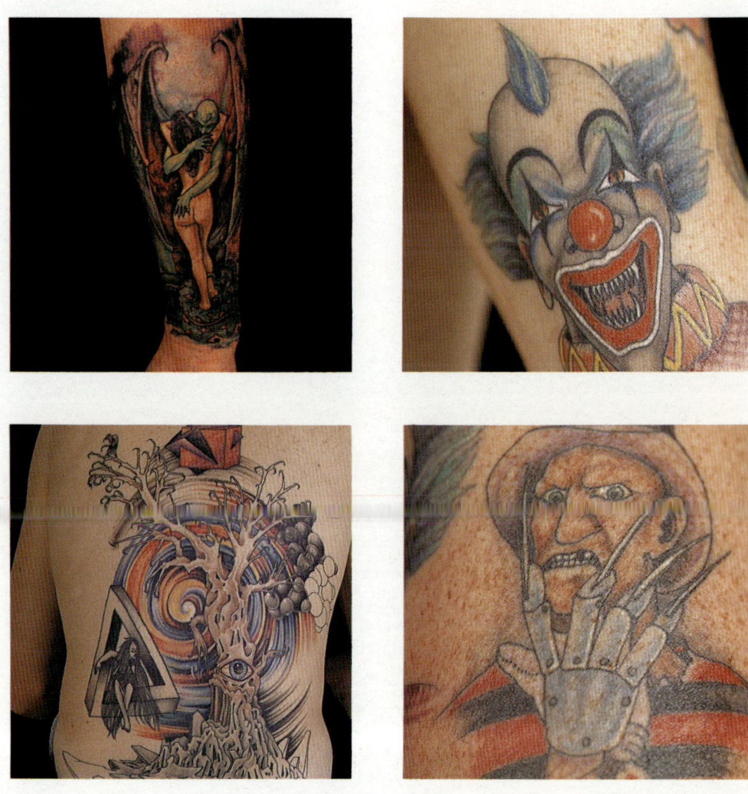

Clockwise, from top left, Sean, service handyman. Design from the Boris Vallejot fantasy book. Mike, 2-stroke mechanic. Phil, artist. Phil's own design, depicts personal conflicts and growth.

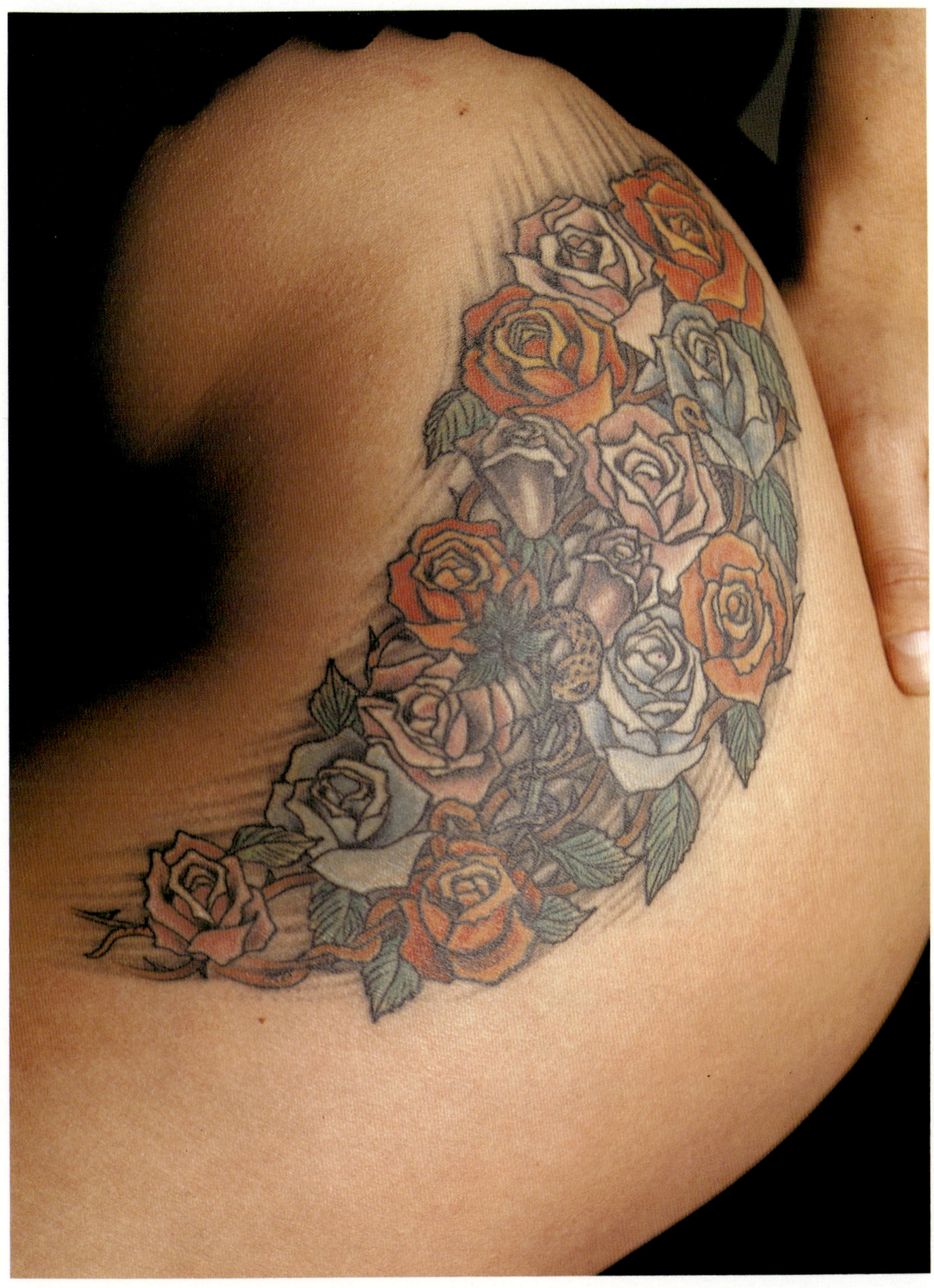

Jackie: detail

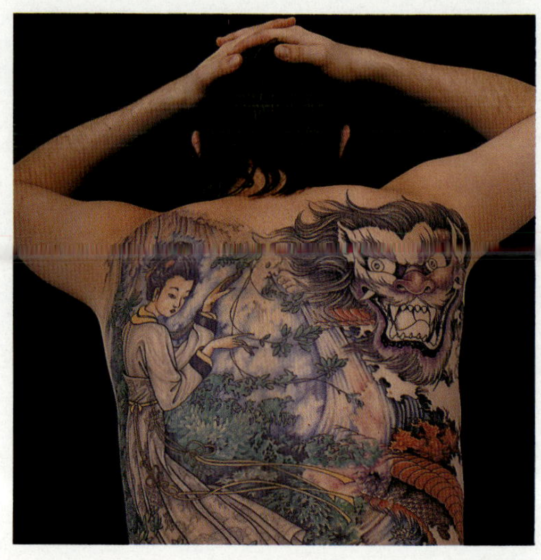

Mark, restaurant manager.

Val, librarian.

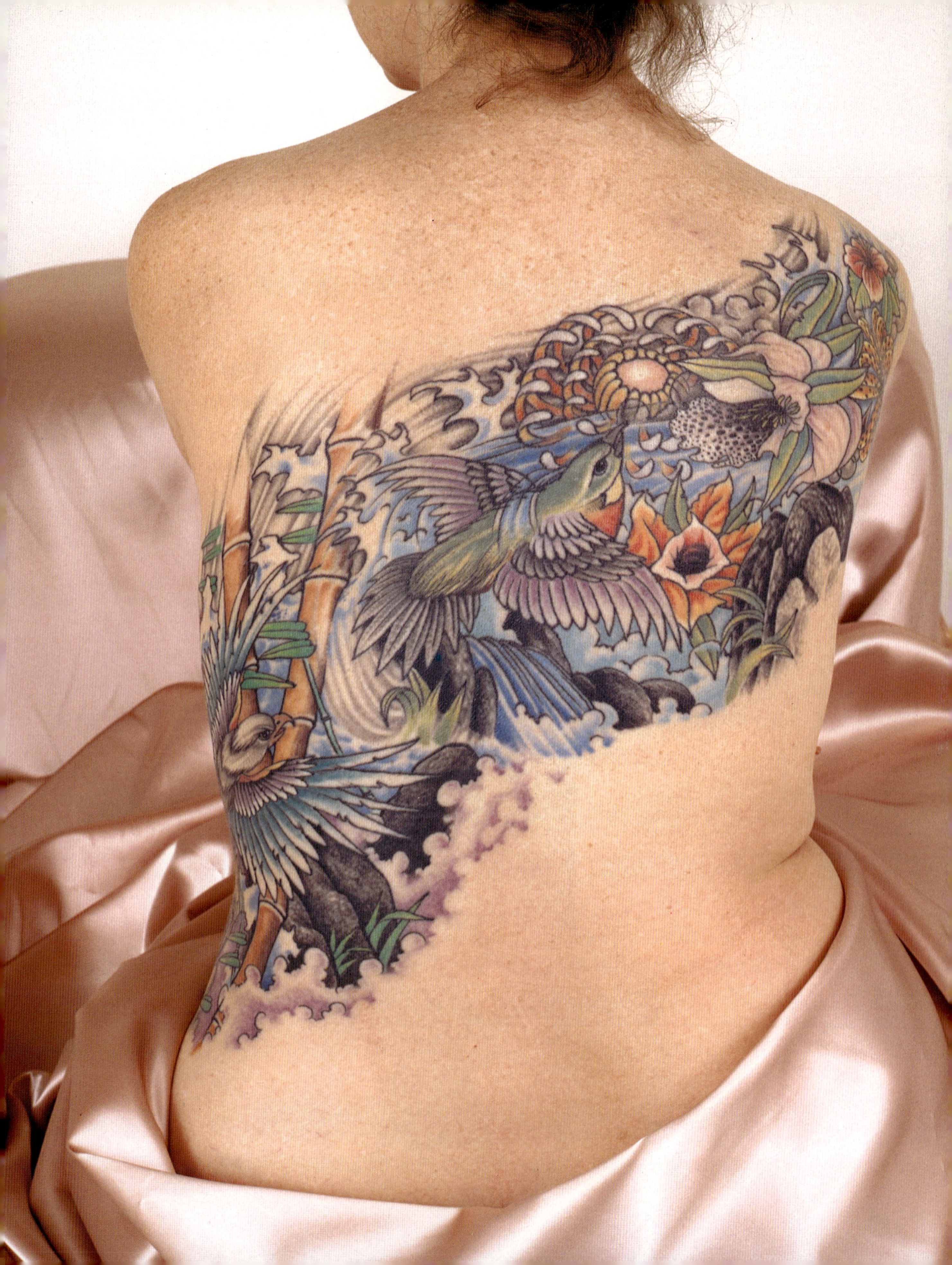

ANOTHER QUIET VIRGO TYPE, Mike is serious about his work. He was very happy to have his work photographed and contacted people for me. Mike also has Samoan tattoos and has had them photographed a number of times. He instructed the tribal tattooist on sterilising his equipment correctly, and the use of modern tattoo inks. Mike is meticulous about recording the work he does and has scrapbooks of photographs. Not only is he fastidious about the way he works, but also the way he manages his studio, situated on one of Auckland's busiest intersections.

Mr Mike works in Otahuhu.

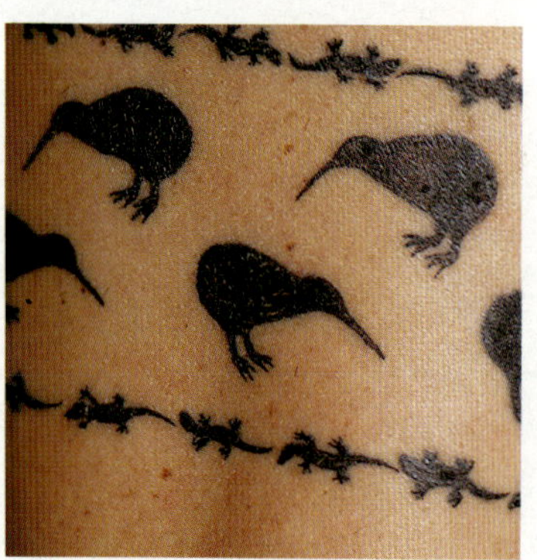

Trevor, barber.

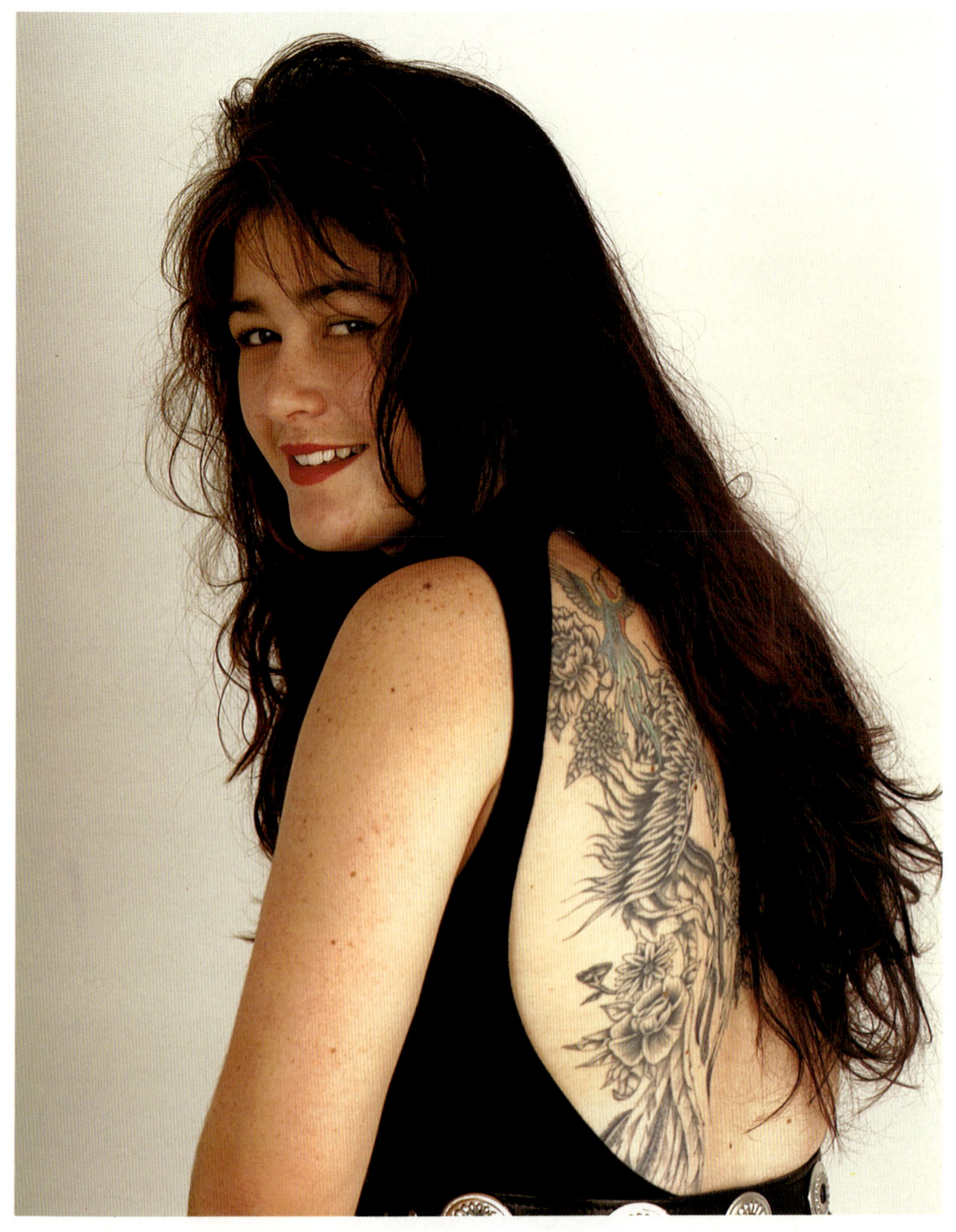

Carmen, hairdresser.

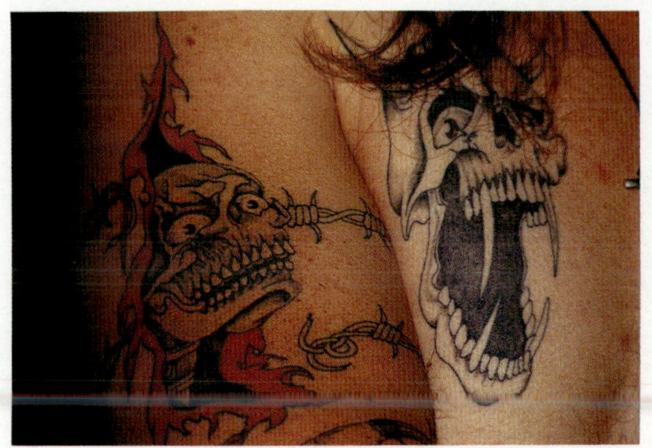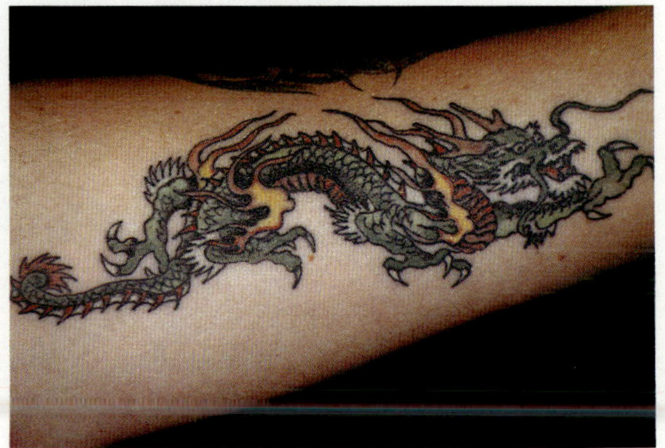

Clint, engineer.

Andrew, salesman.

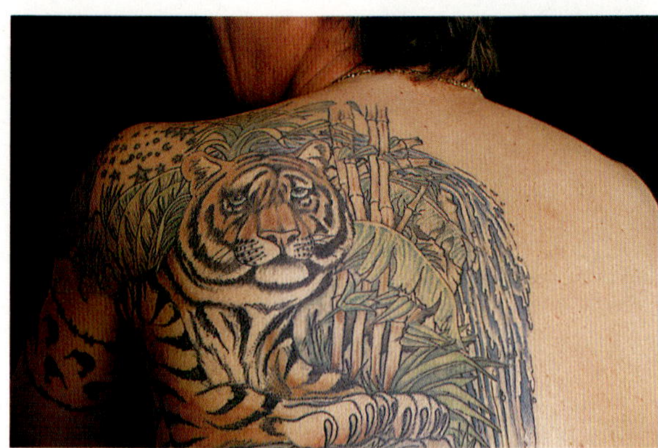 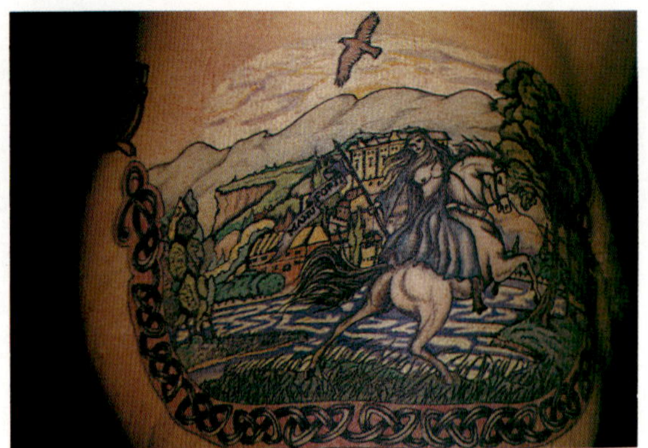

Trev, barber.

Graeme, accountant.

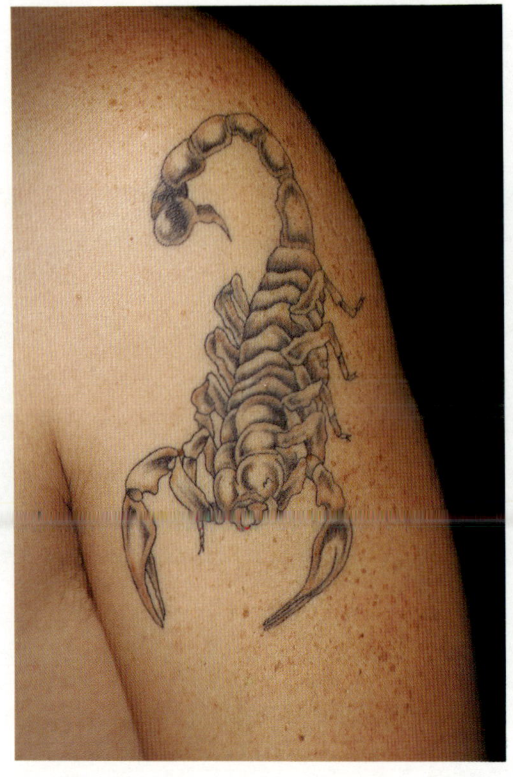

Clint.

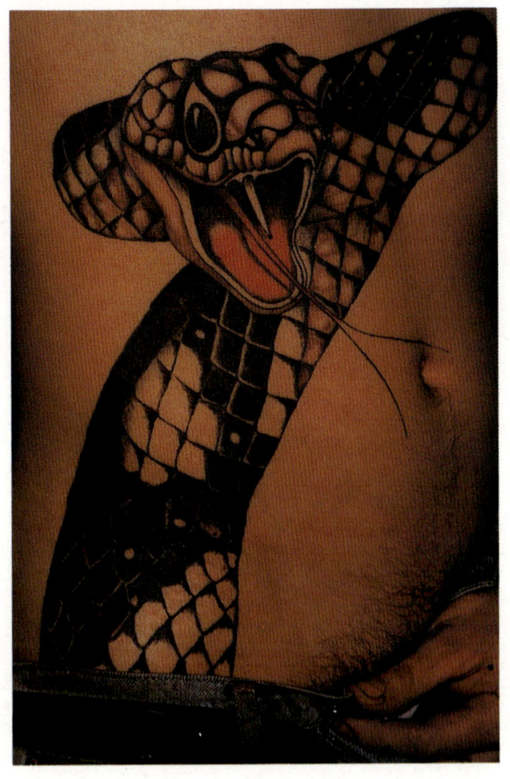

Paddy.

THIS IS A VERY INTERESTING PARTNERSHIP, where mother and son work together as tattoo artists. Jude and Sarge have been in the business 20 years and nine years respectively. Sarge's late father taught Jude, and Sarge, who caught the bug at age four, learnt from both parents. Their studio is vast, incorporating bikes, T-shirts, flags, etc.

This establishment exudes the family bond that ties them together, with the influence of their former teacher still very much in evidence.

Jude and Sarge work in Palmerston North.

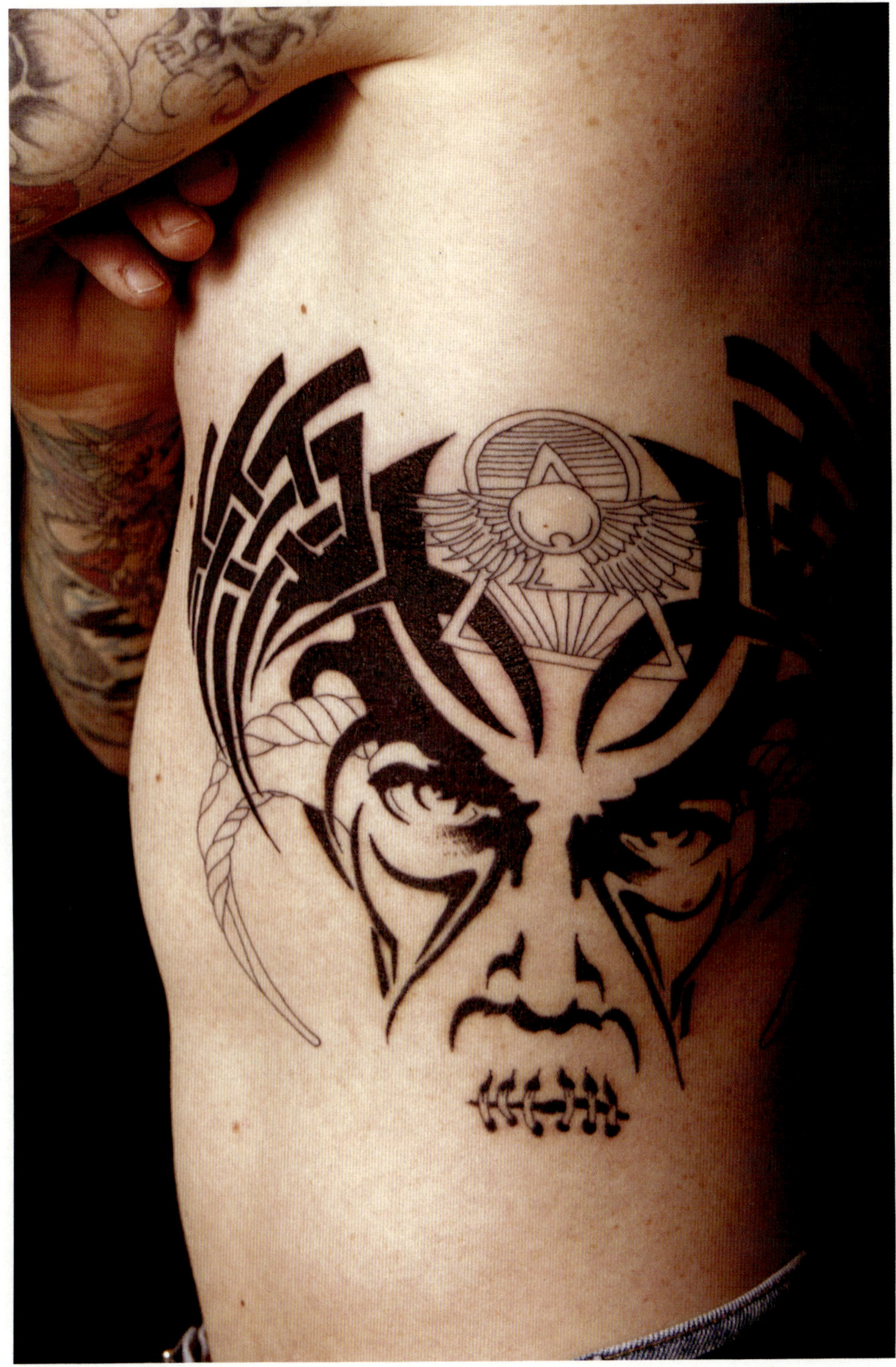

Dave.

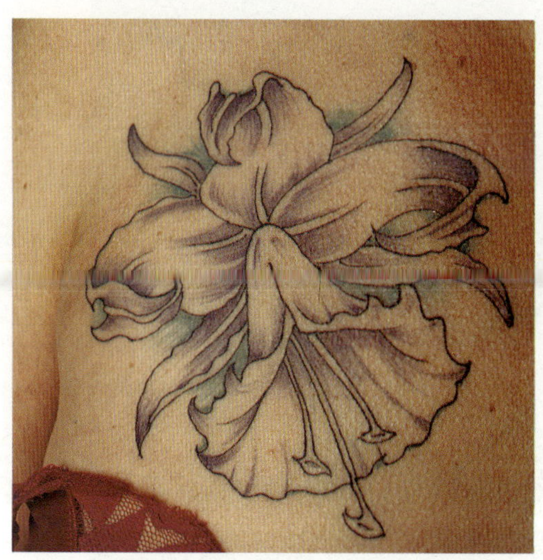 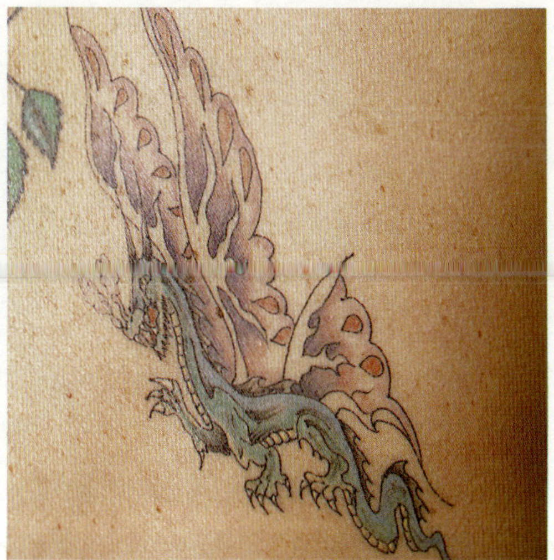

Sandy: the orchids were tattooed
in memory of her mother.

Sonja: likes tribal strength to outline
feminine flowers and birds.

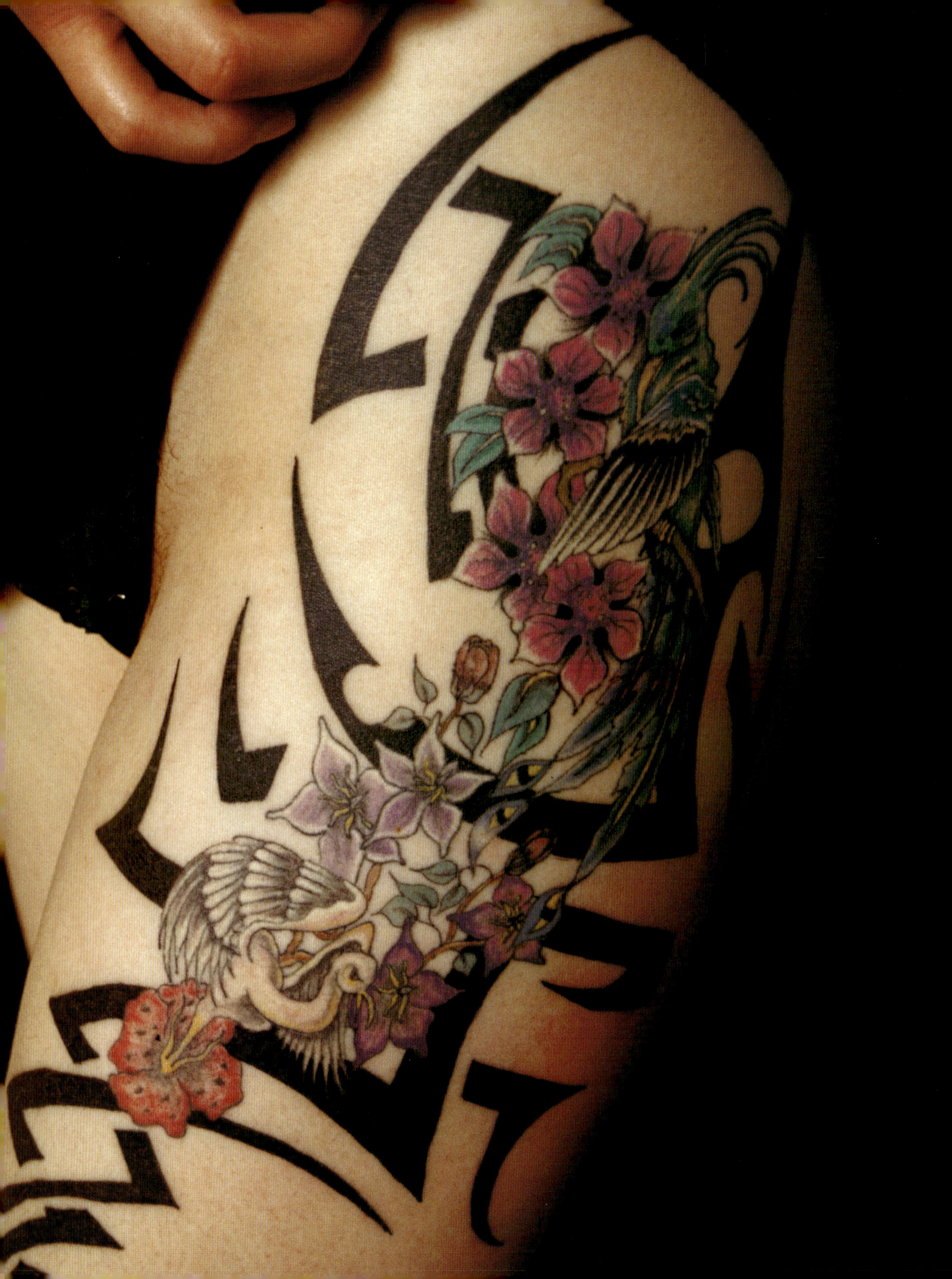

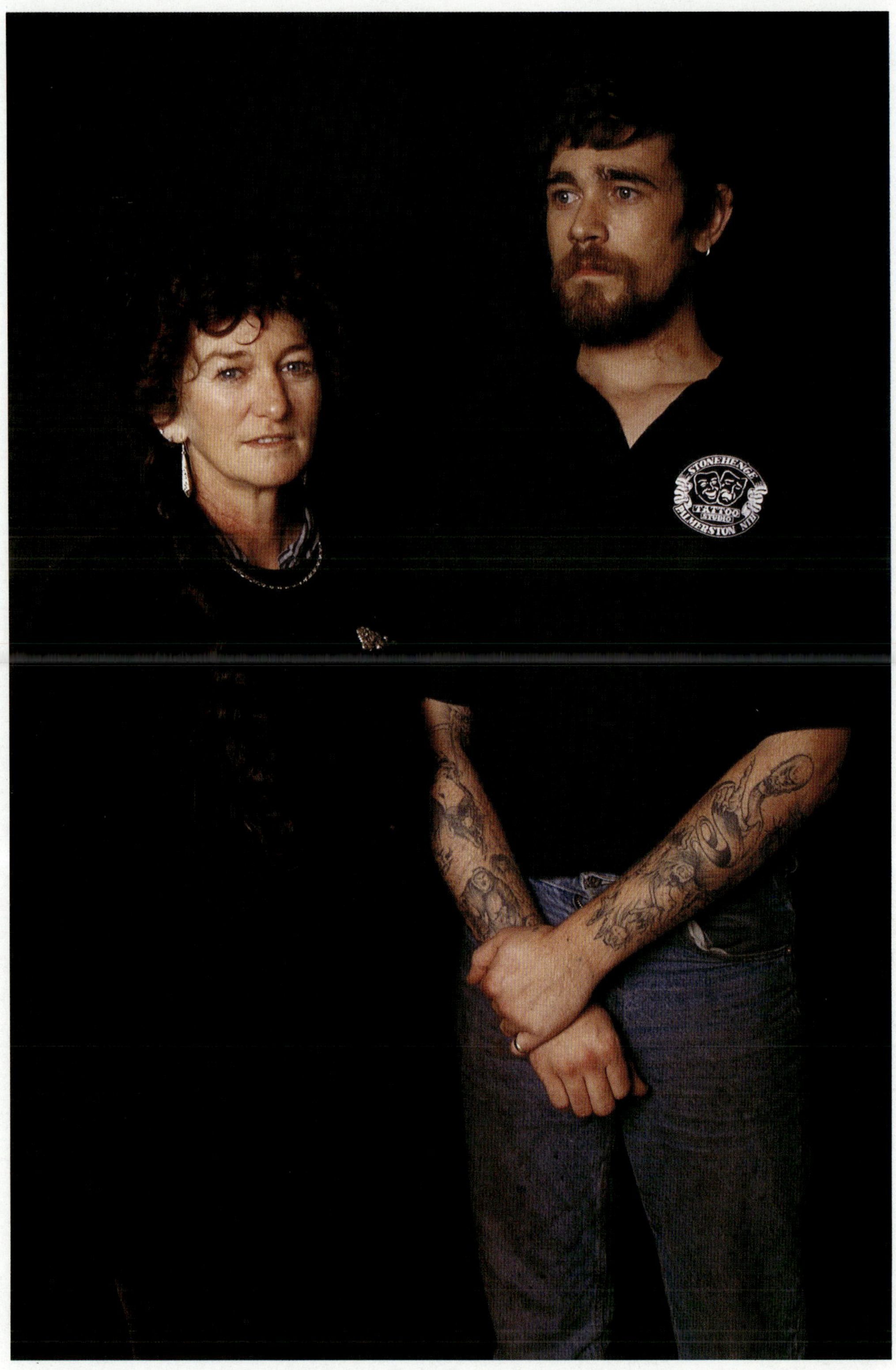

Jude and Sarge, mother and son tattooists.

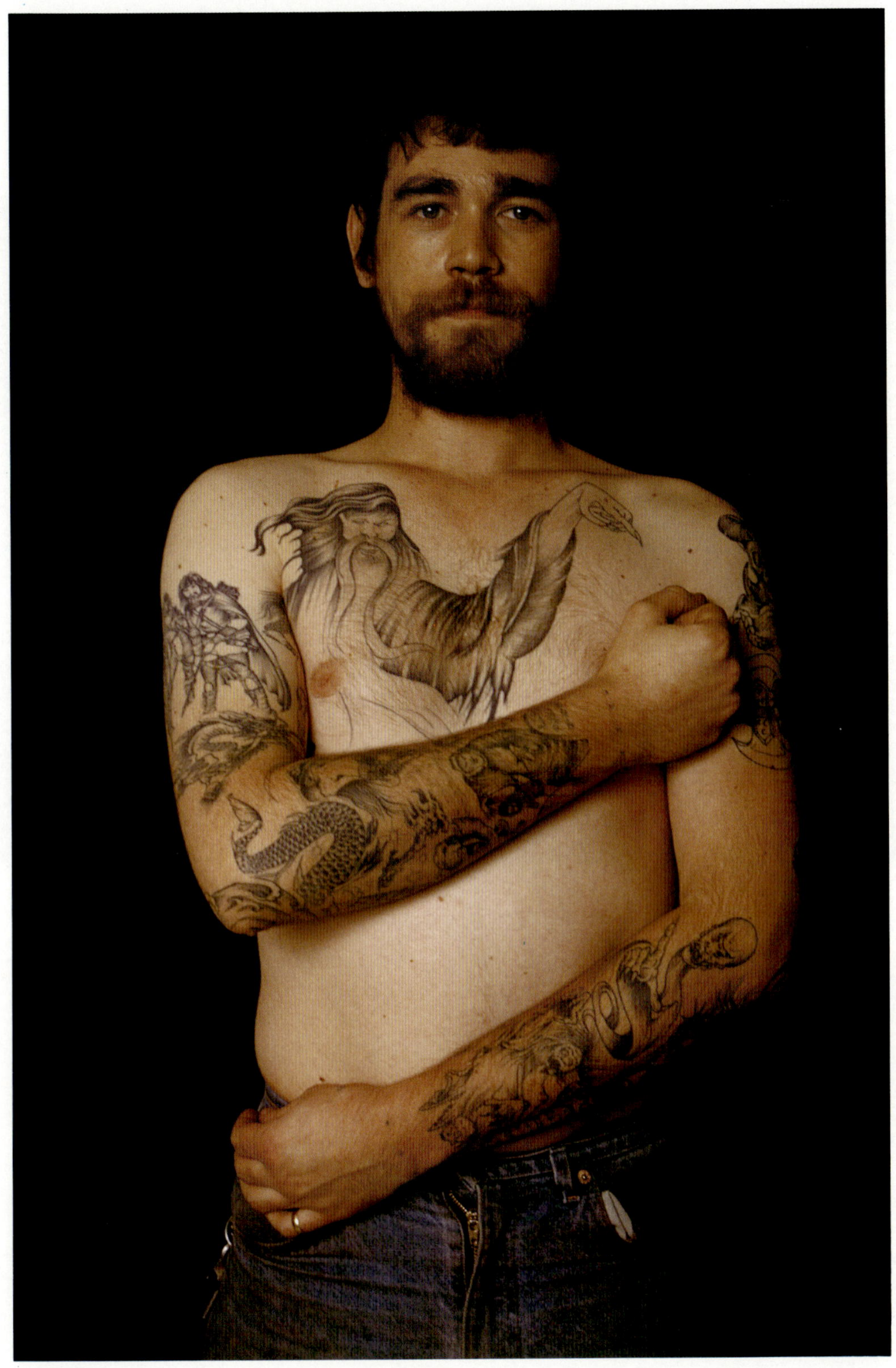

Sarge, work by Jude.

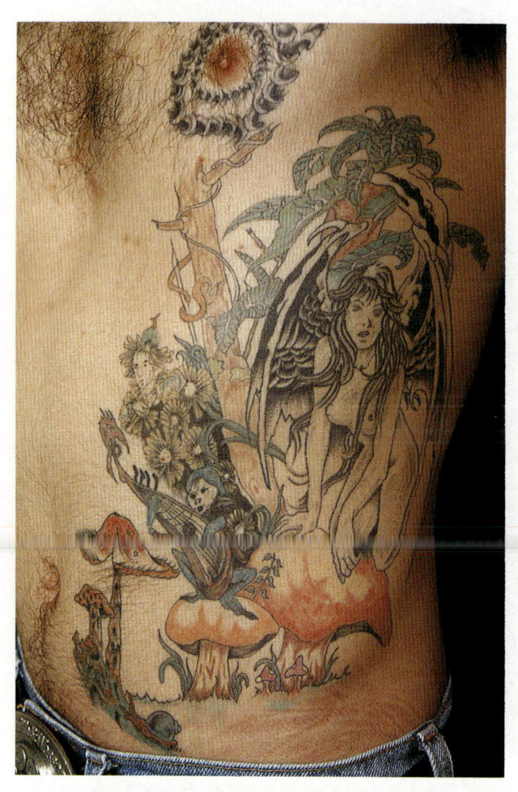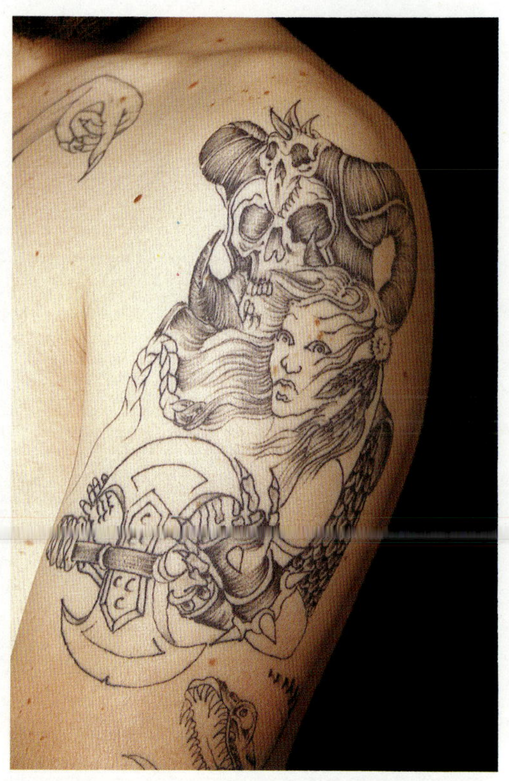

Dean.

Sarge, work by Jude.

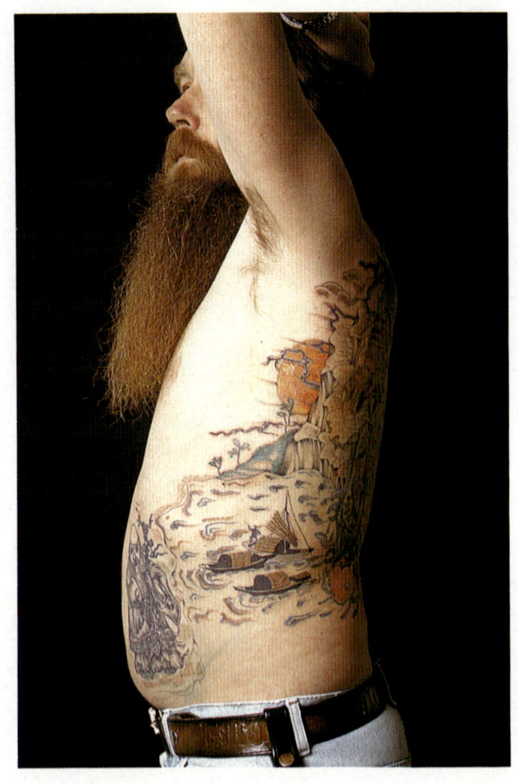

Paul, married to Sandy.

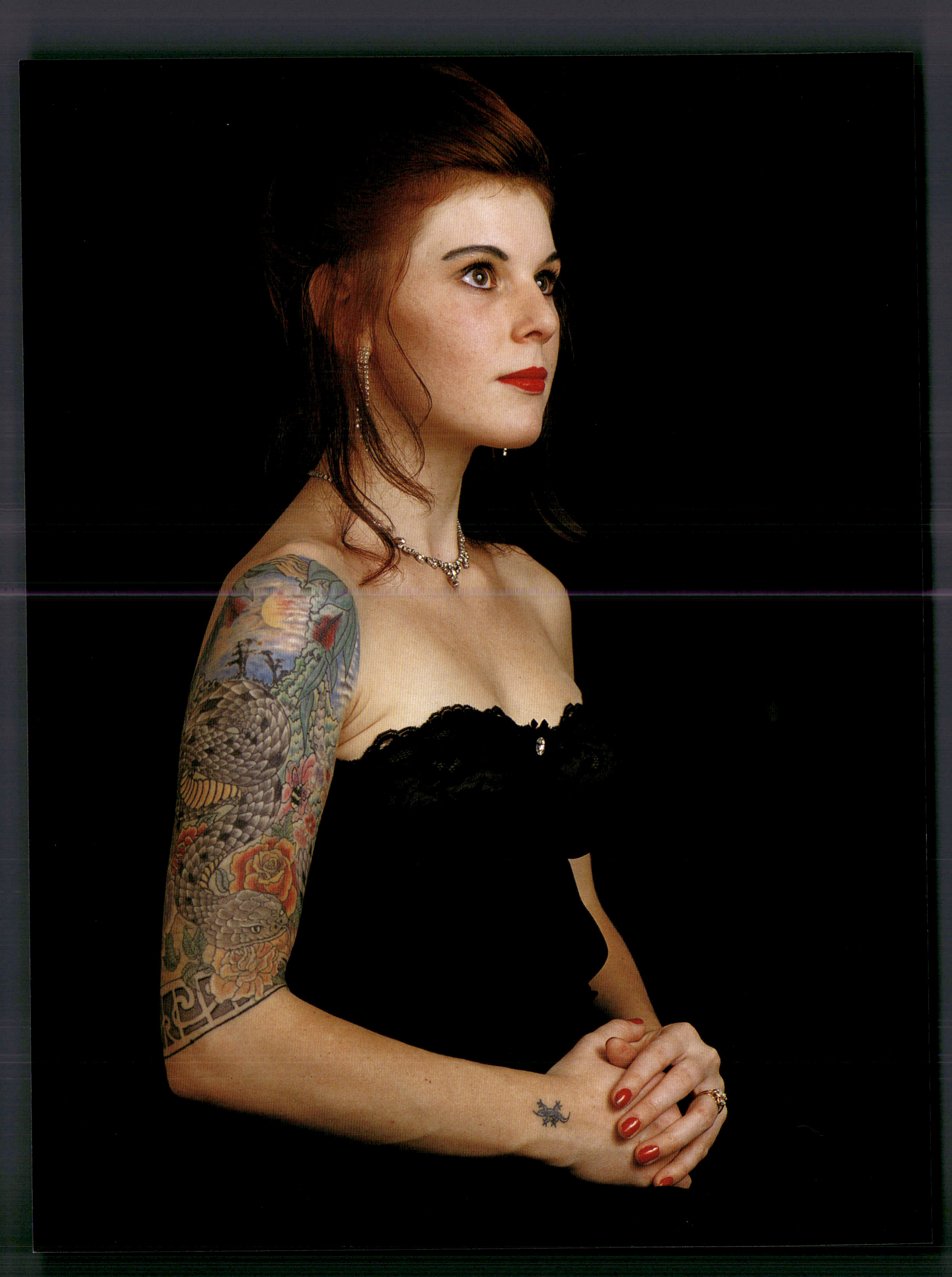

GRAHAM IS LAID-BACK and easygoing. His studio in central Auckland is spacious and airy, with polished bare wood floors and a loft ceiling. His clients are also his friends and so there was no problem gathering them together for a photo session. He has a flair for portraiture and has a tattoo of Marilyn Monroe on his leg which he did himself. He also specialises in Celtic and tribal designs.

   Graham and his partner Debbie were invited to Amsterdam to work with top European tattoo artists at the 1993 convention.

Graham Cavanagh works in Auckland.

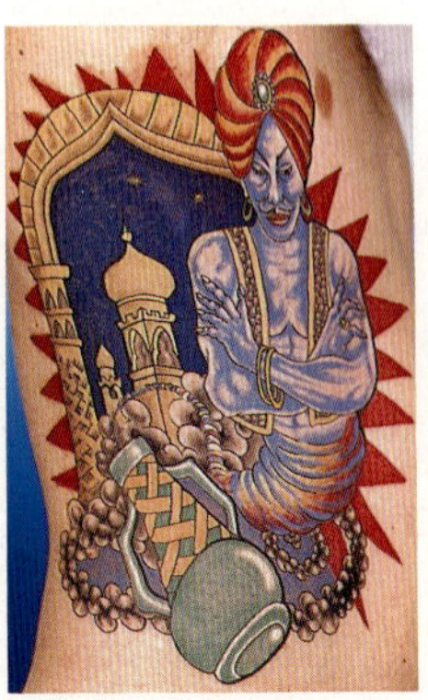

Debbie, partner/assistant.

Andrew: 'Bob in the Bottle'

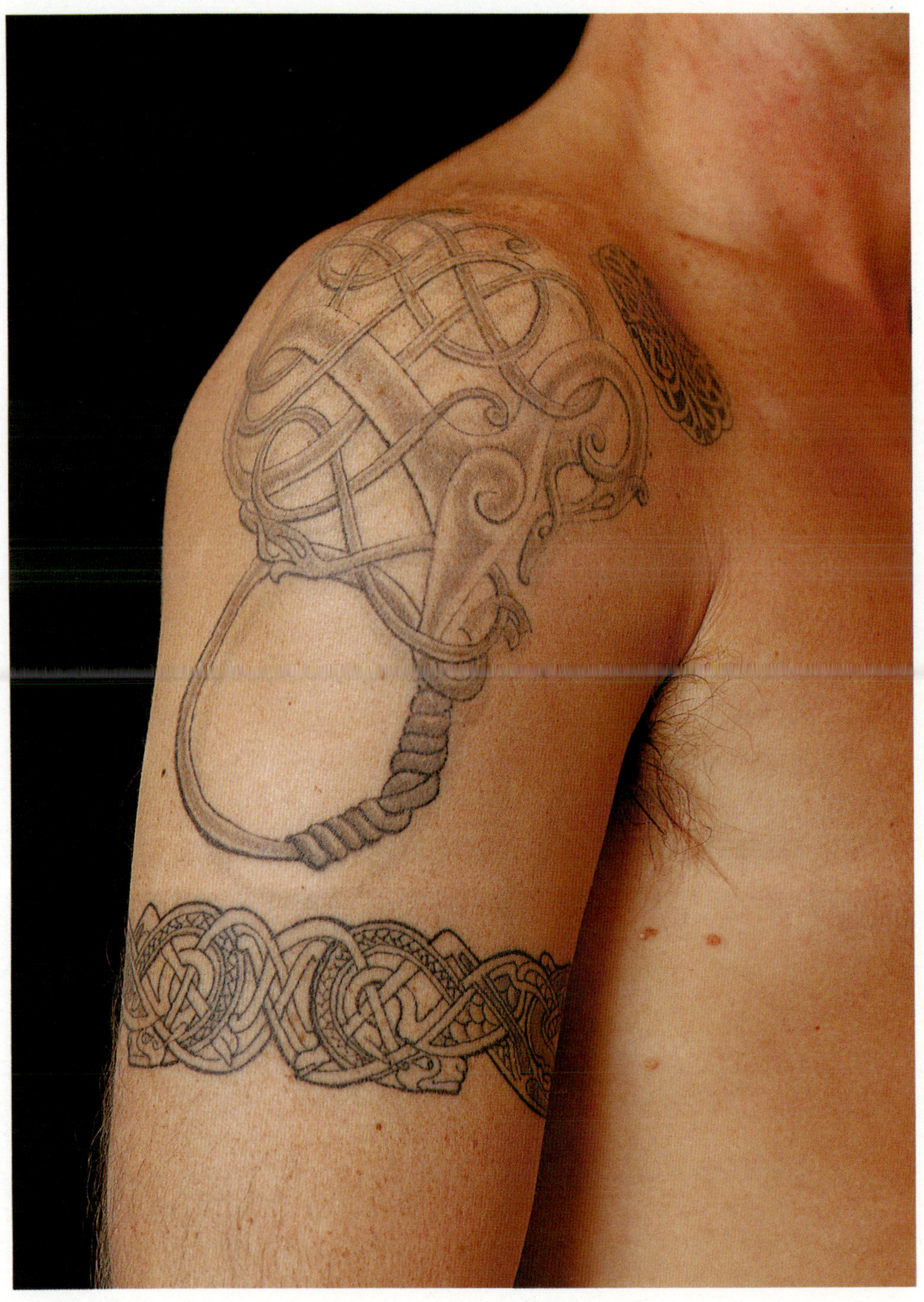

Craig.

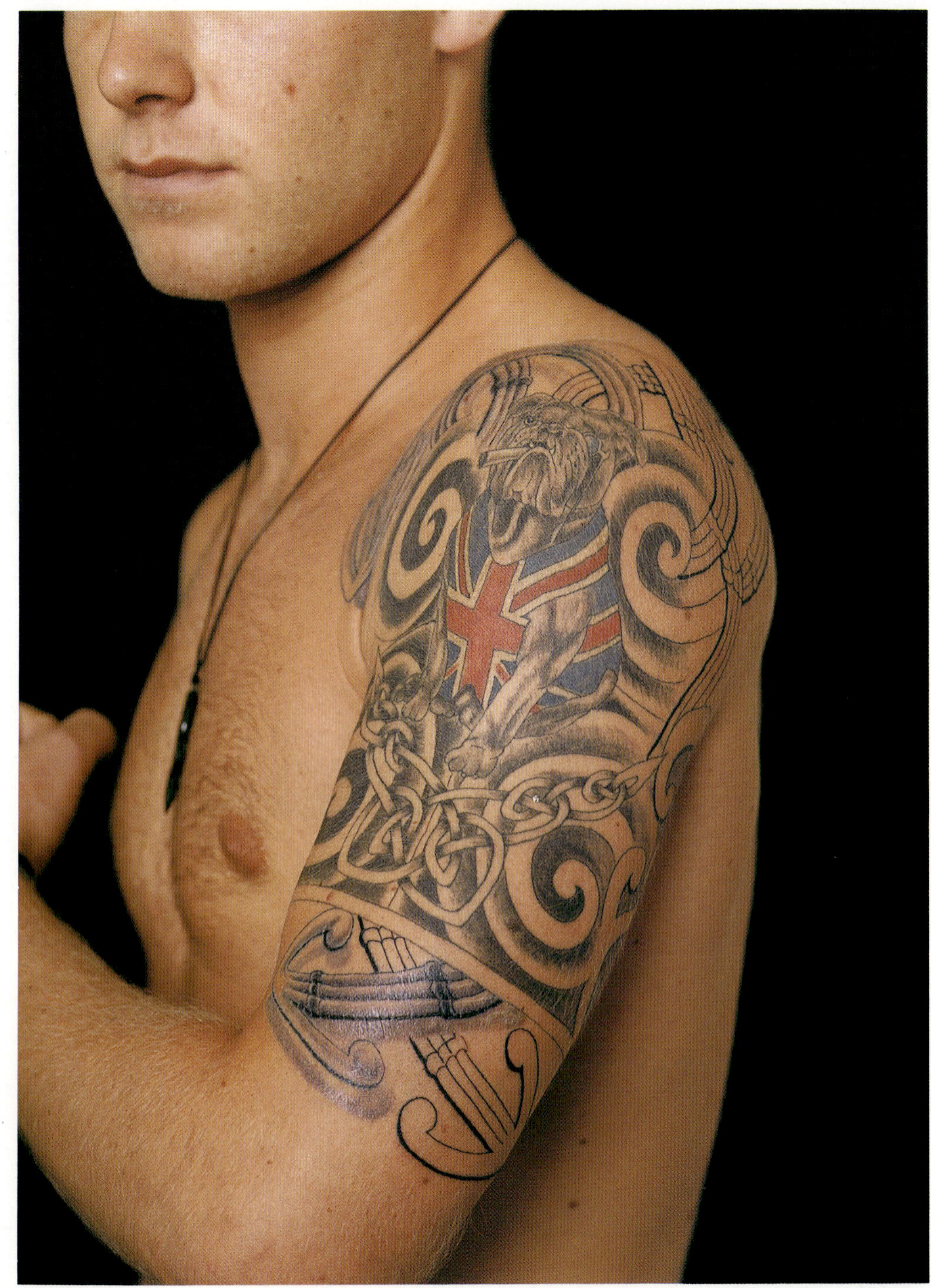

Aaron.

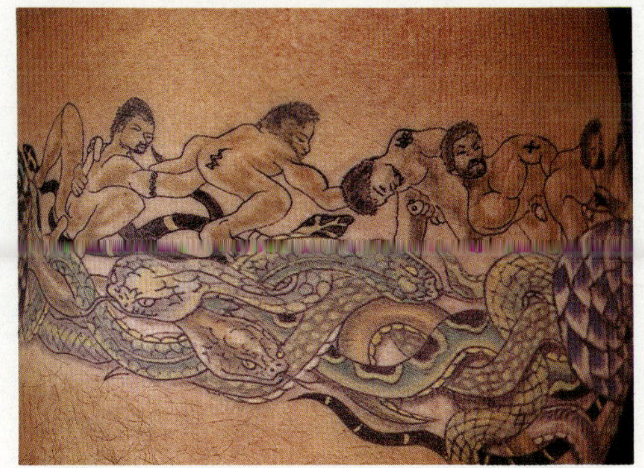

Keith.

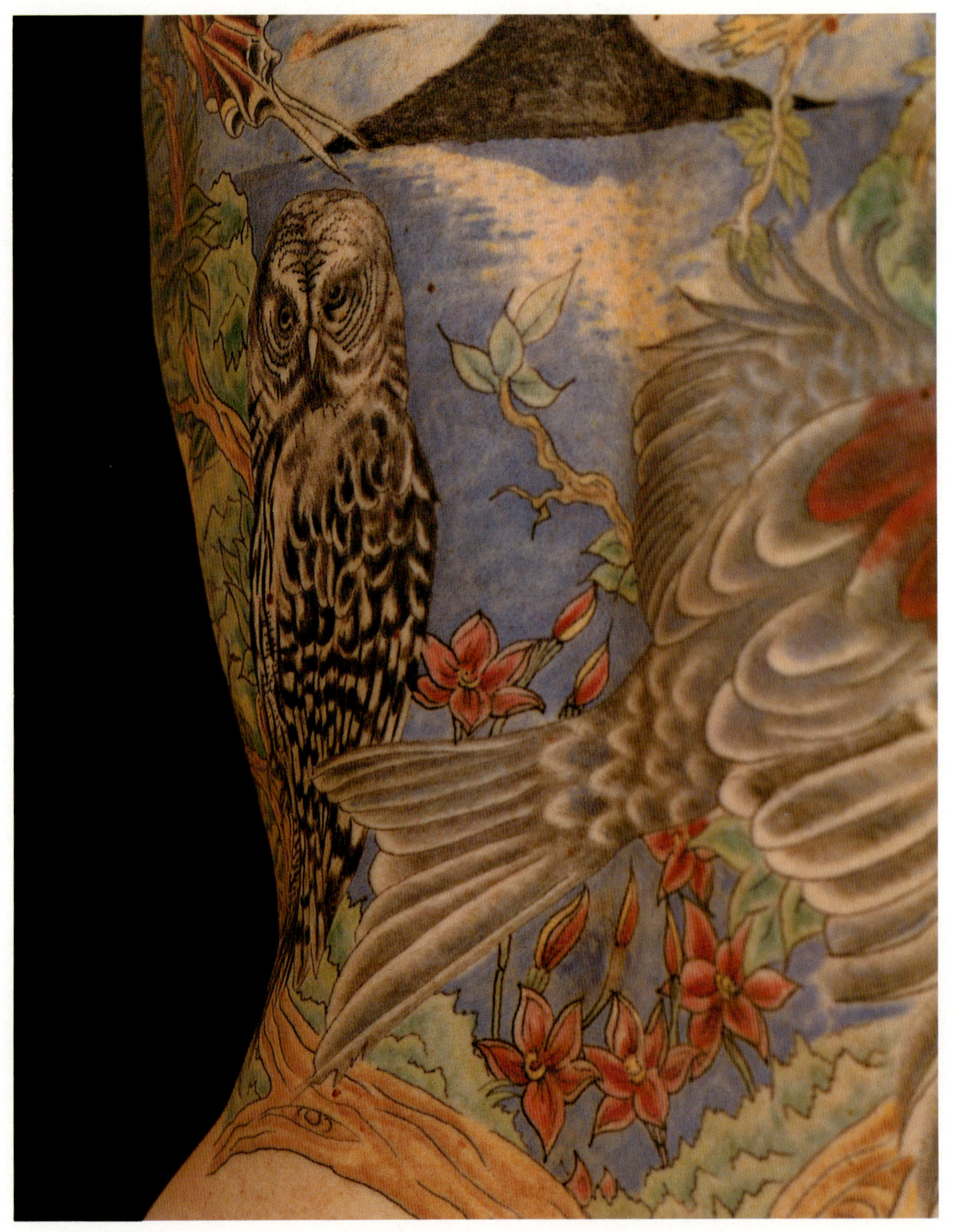

Adelle, secretary.

# KEN MILLER

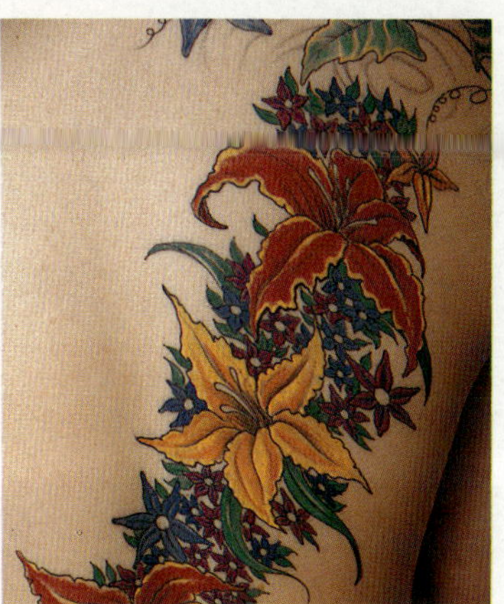

Caroline, baker.

Nicci: Medusa tattoo took
3 hours, completed in one sitting.

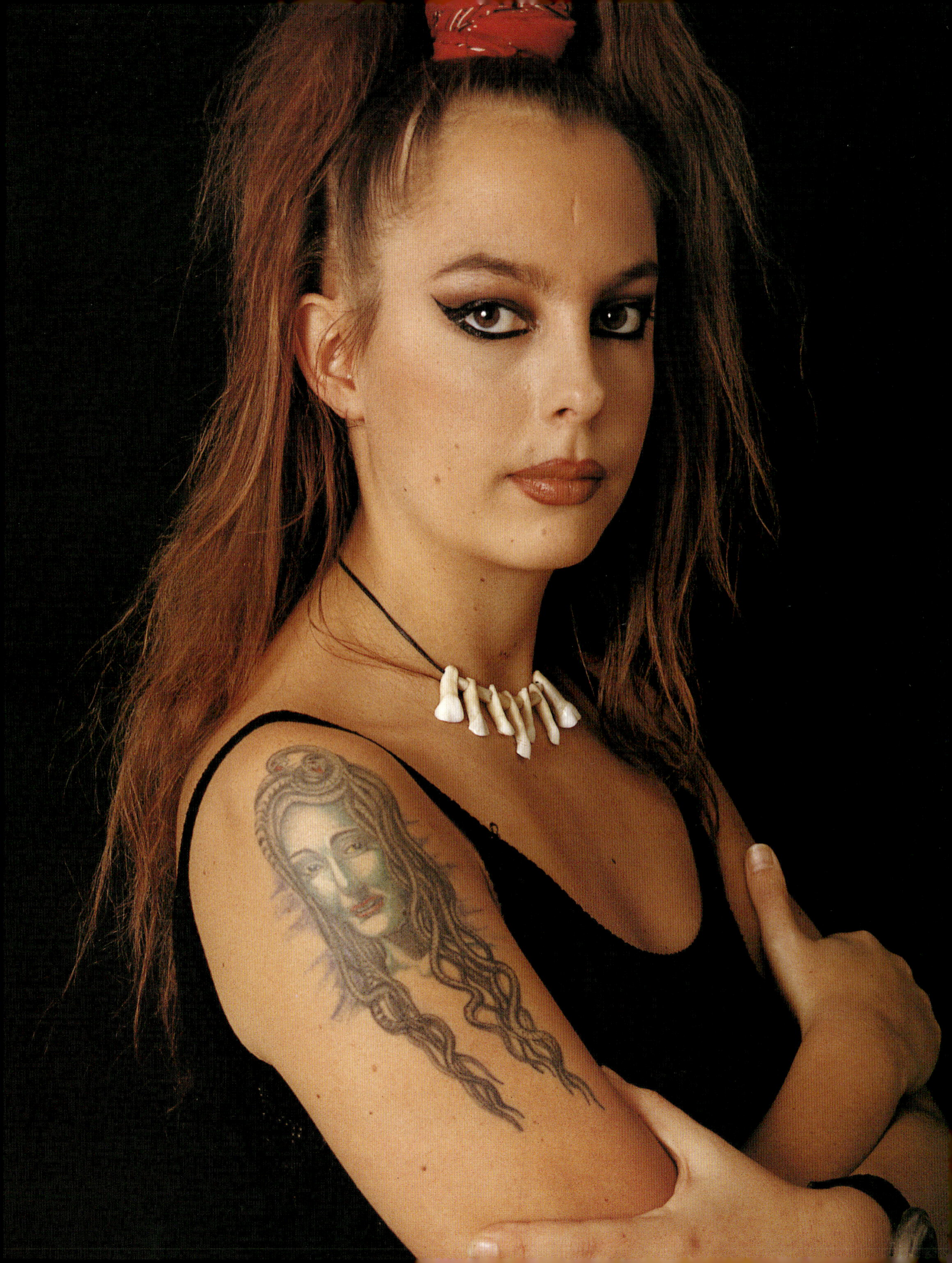

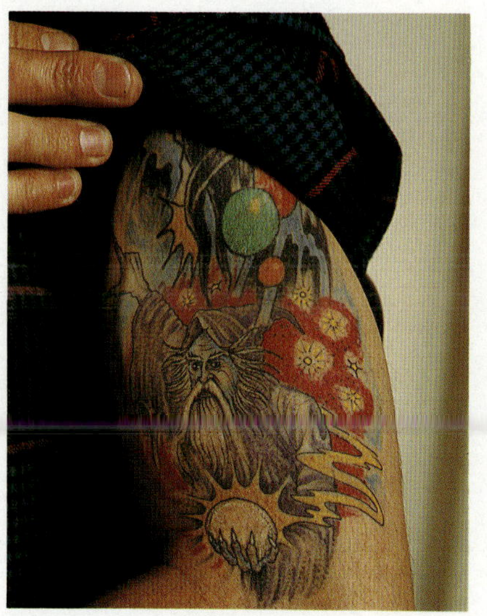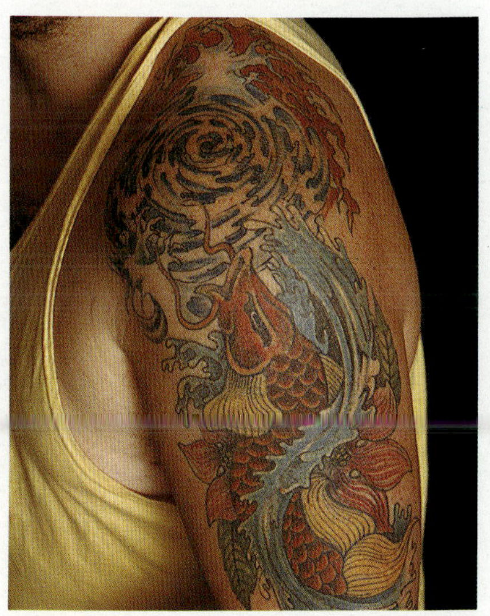

Perry, member of the Napier Tattoo Club.

Stu, tattoo artist.

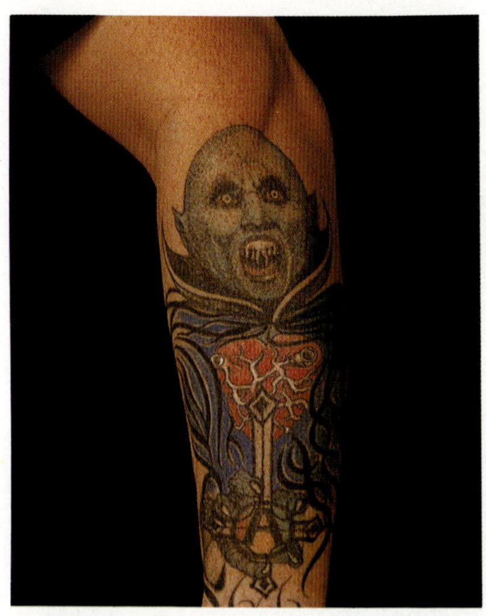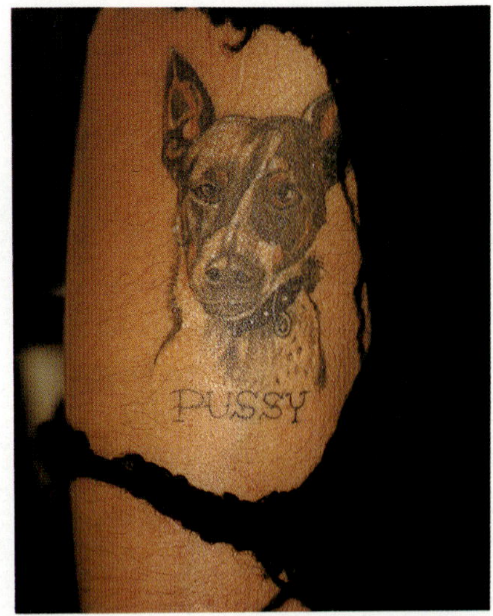

David, market co-ordinator.

Carl: tattoo of 6-year-old dog Pussy.

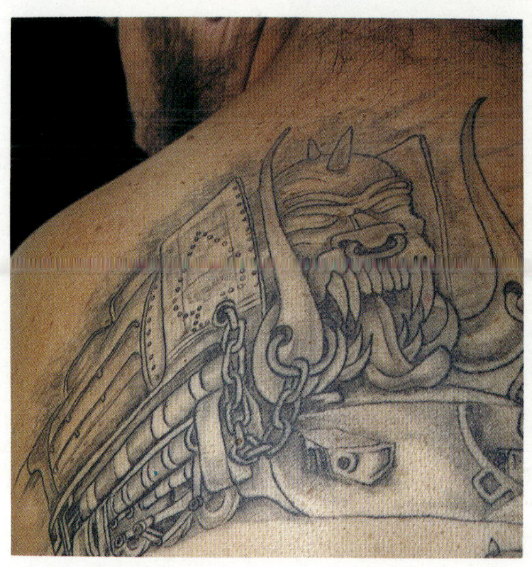 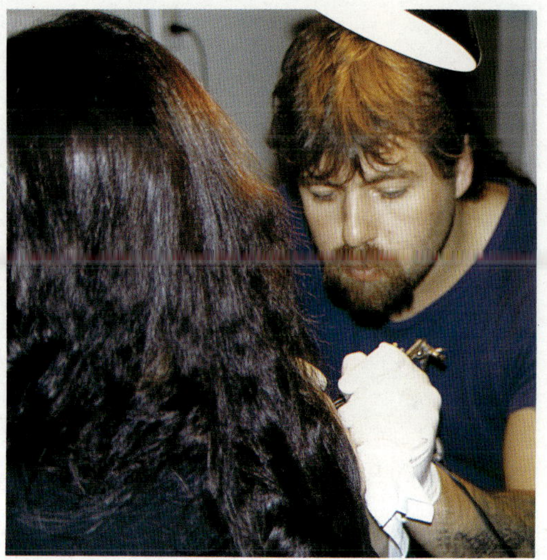

Stephen.

Ken at work.

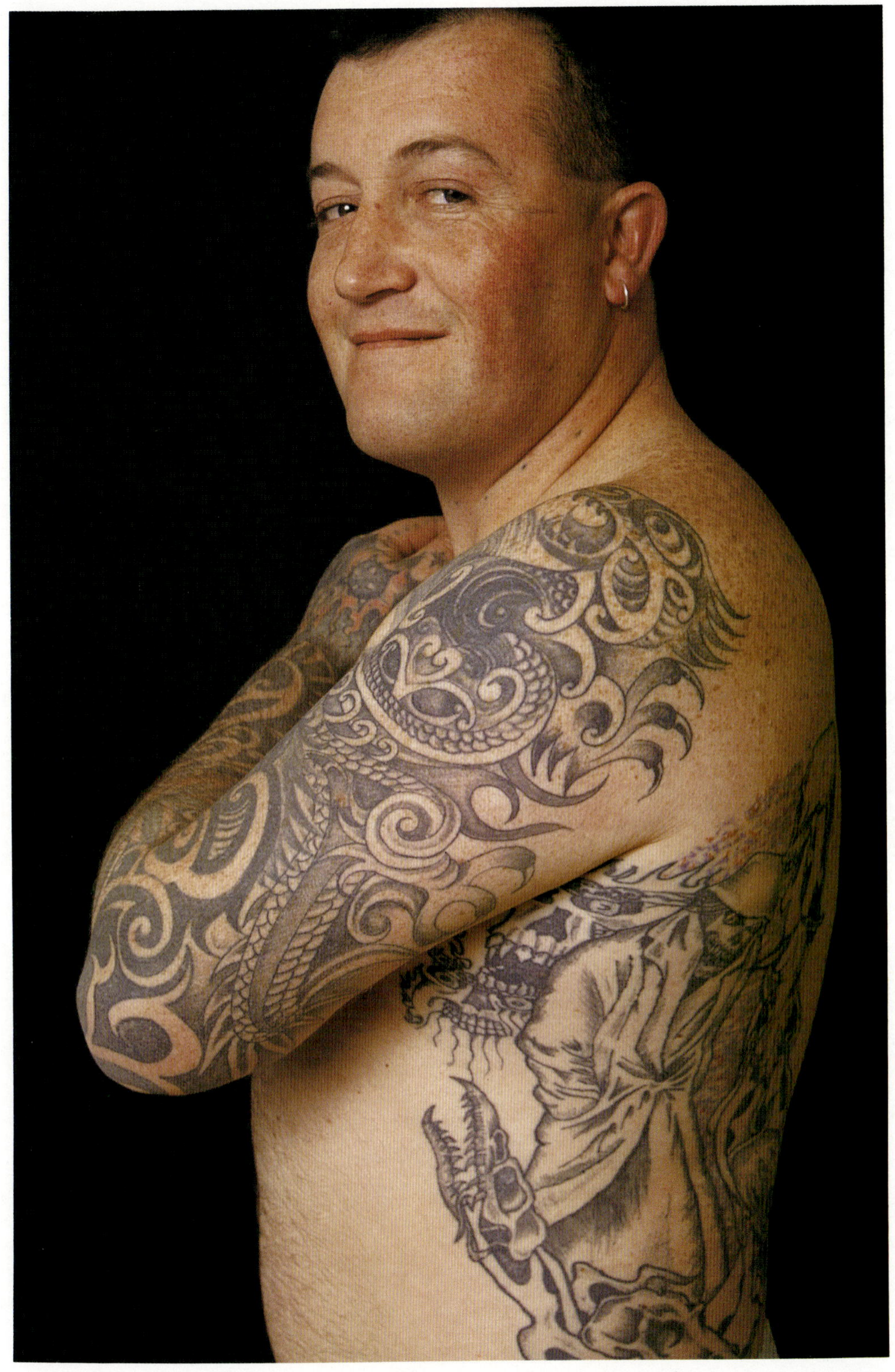

Rob, commercial fisherman.

# A D R I A N   J U R Y

ADRIAN, A TALL SKINNY MAN with long brown hair, eats, sleeps and breathes tattooing. He works from home and supports a young family. Other tattooists and styles don't seem to faze him at all — Adrian follows his own direction, uninfluenced by his peers. Though he has no regular contact with other tattoo artists, this man is full of life and jokes constantly, talking non-stop, ribbing his clients and arranging parties.

He is heavily involved with the Napier Tattoo Club which has a very strong following; many of the patrons are his customers and friends. This personable character has the moral support of his long-suffering wife Cheryl. They have a close partnership which works. Animated about everything, but especially tattooing, Adrian's enthusiasm rubs off on those around him.

Adrian Jury works in Napier.

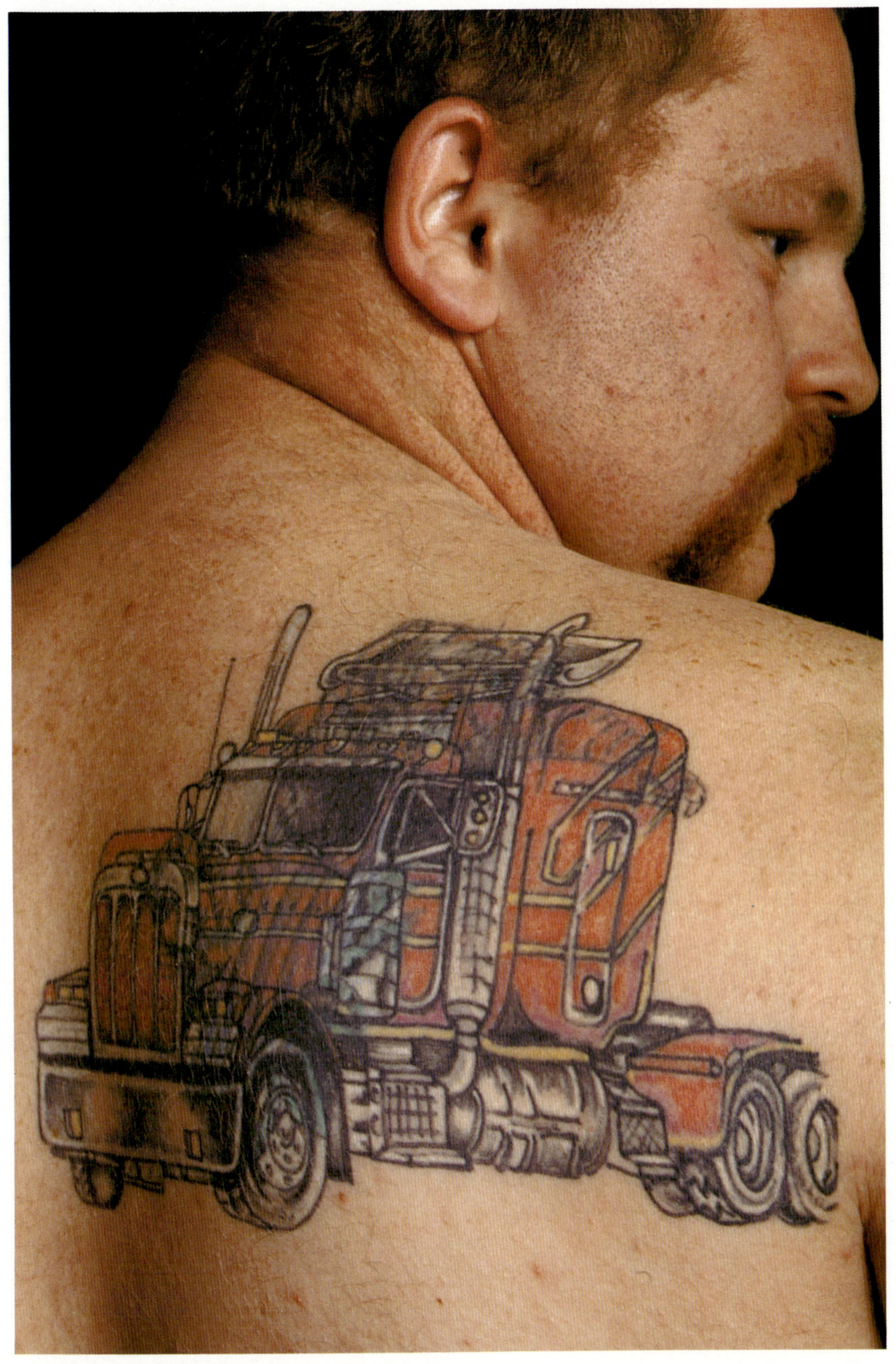

Barrie, works for trucking firm.

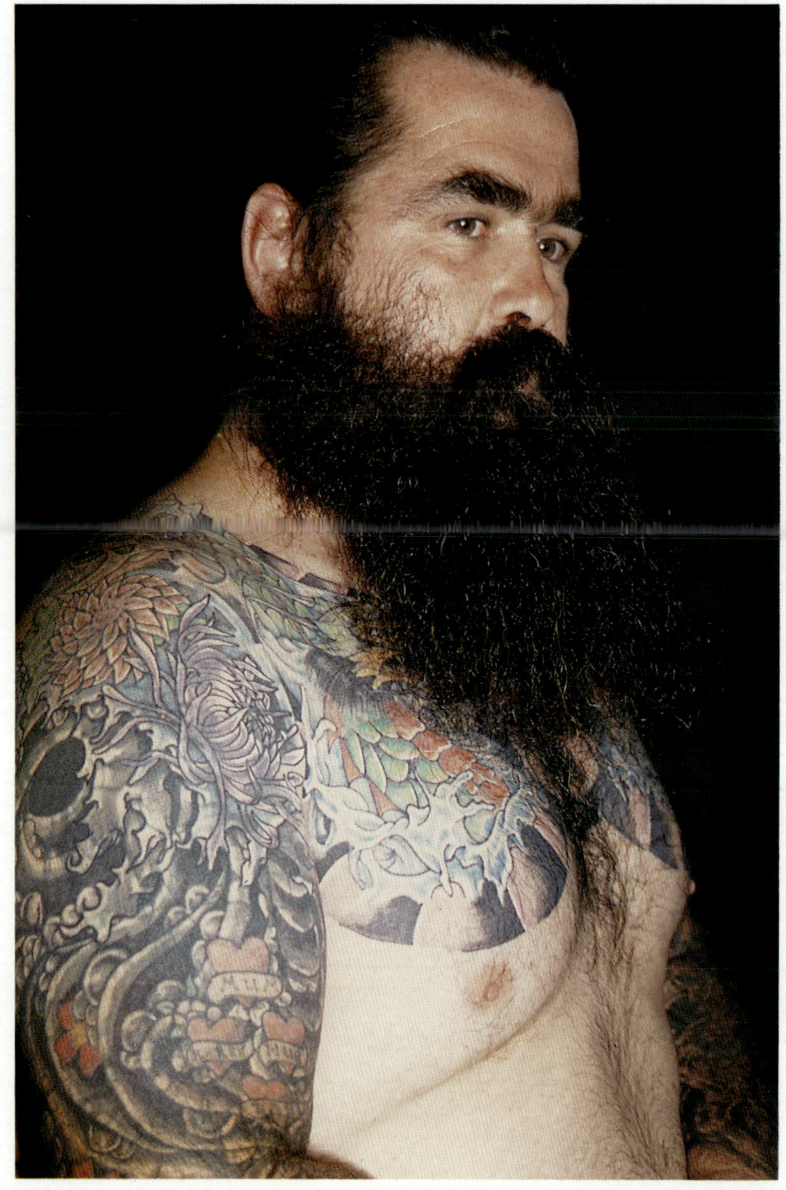

Huggie.

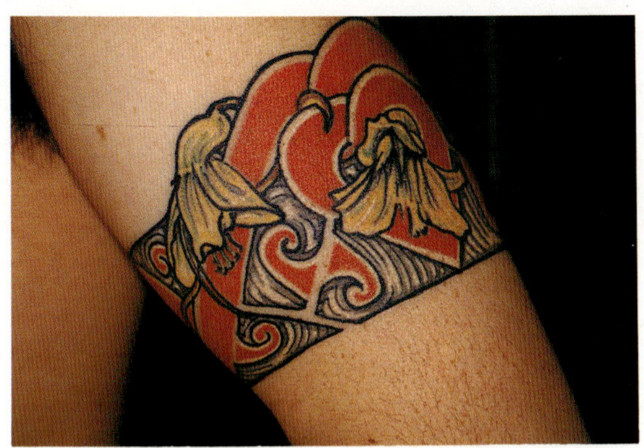 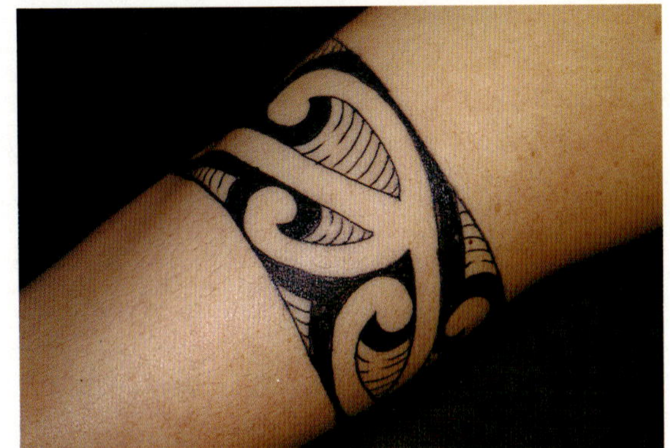

Paul.

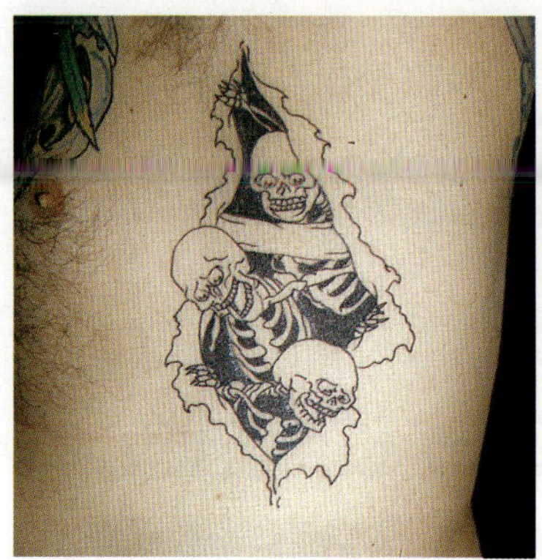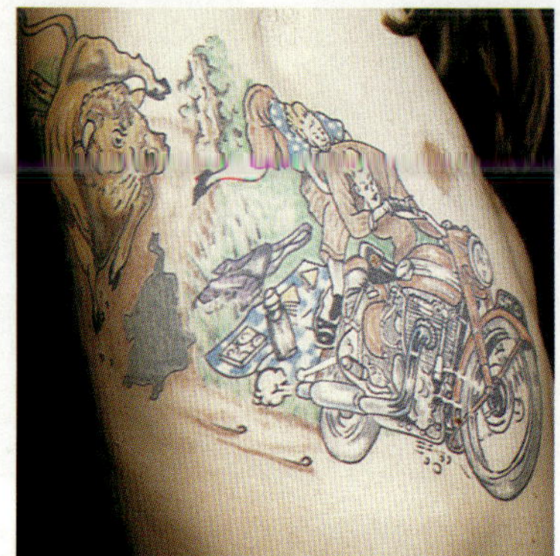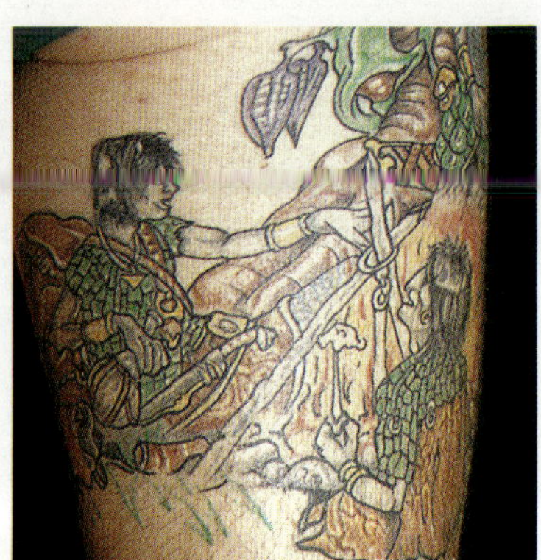

Dennis.

Alan: design from old *Triumph* Magazine.

Alan P.

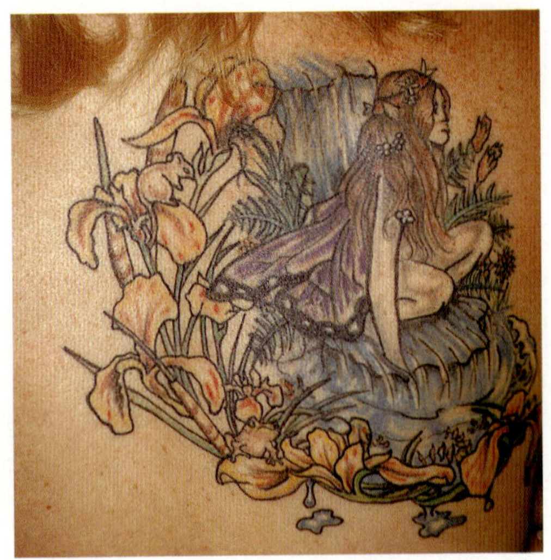

Cheryl.

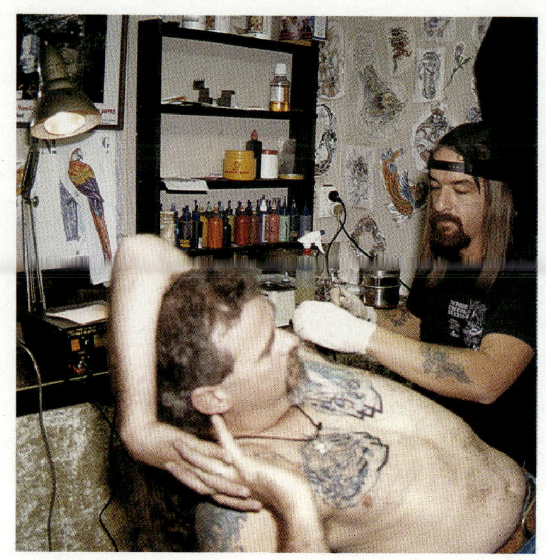

Adrian Jury at work.

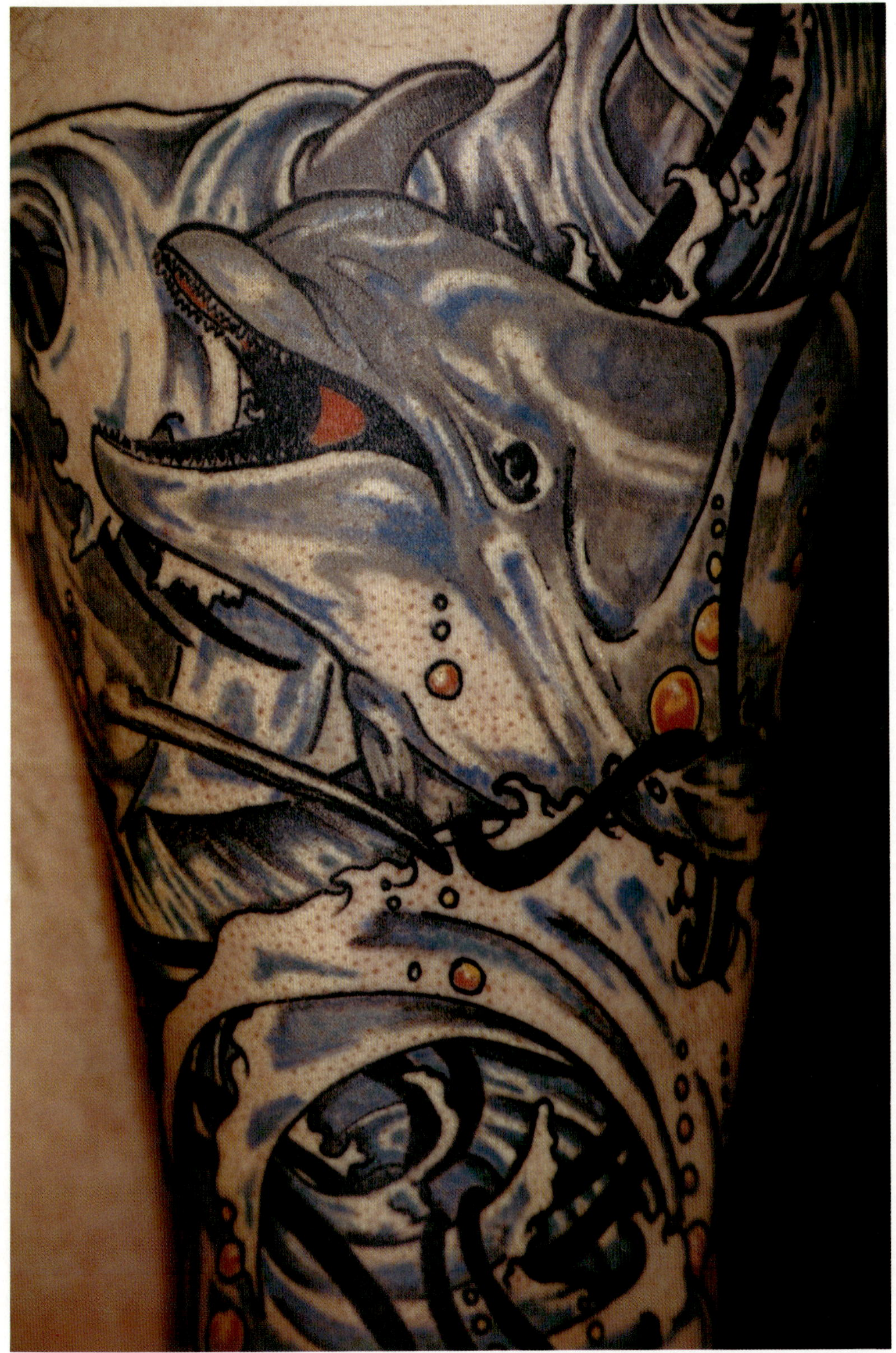

Warren.

STEVE IS SLIM and wiry, of Chinese/Samoan descent. He wears his Samoan tattoos with pride, but displays them only on special occassions and would not allow me to photograph them.

He works in Auckland city with Merv O'Connor. His clients are of an itinerant nature and are difficult to track down once Steve has completed their work. They are off overseas or to other parts of the country returning only when the urge for more tattoos dictates.

Steve has a passion for big work, of oriental design.

Wayne, butcher.

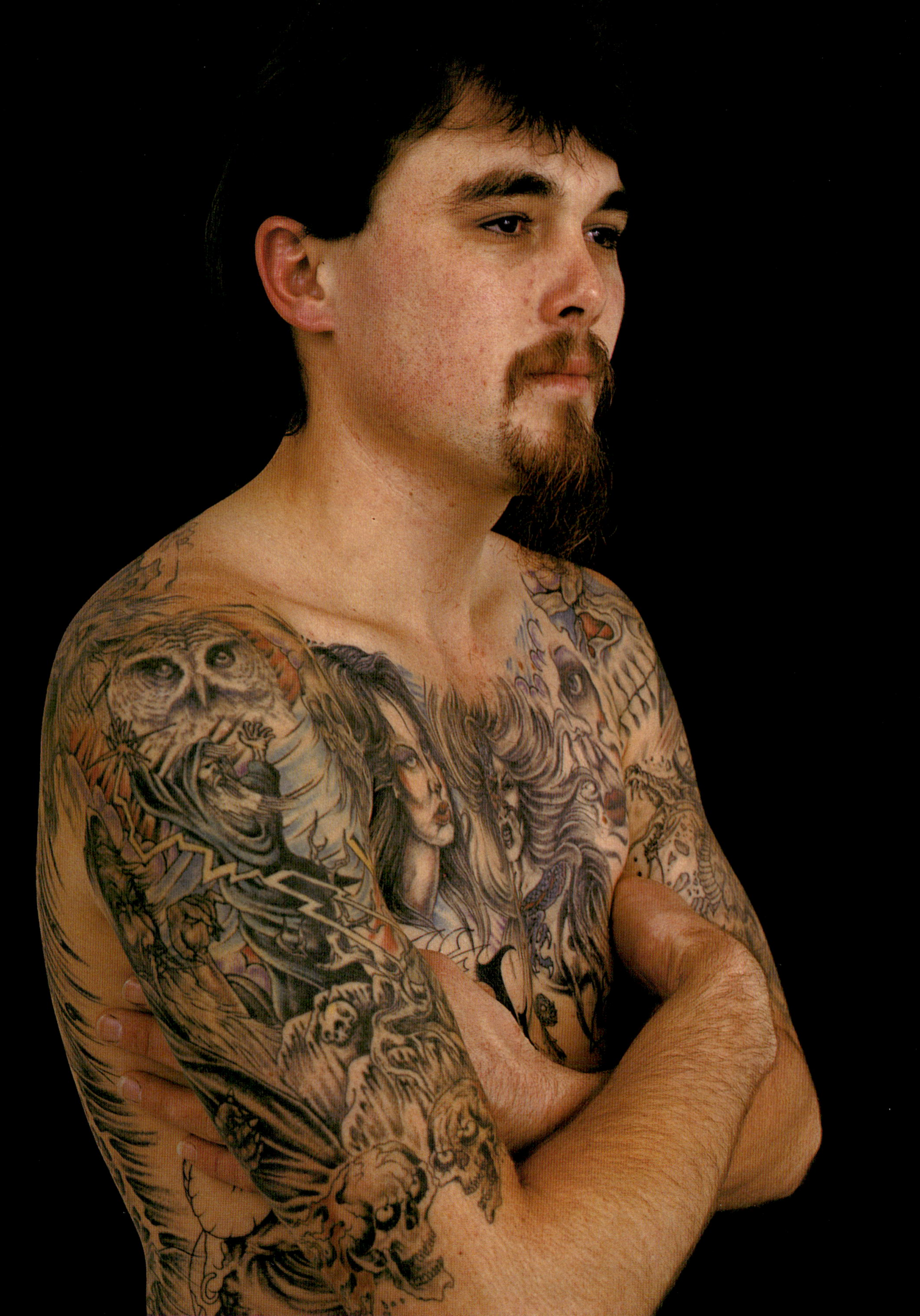

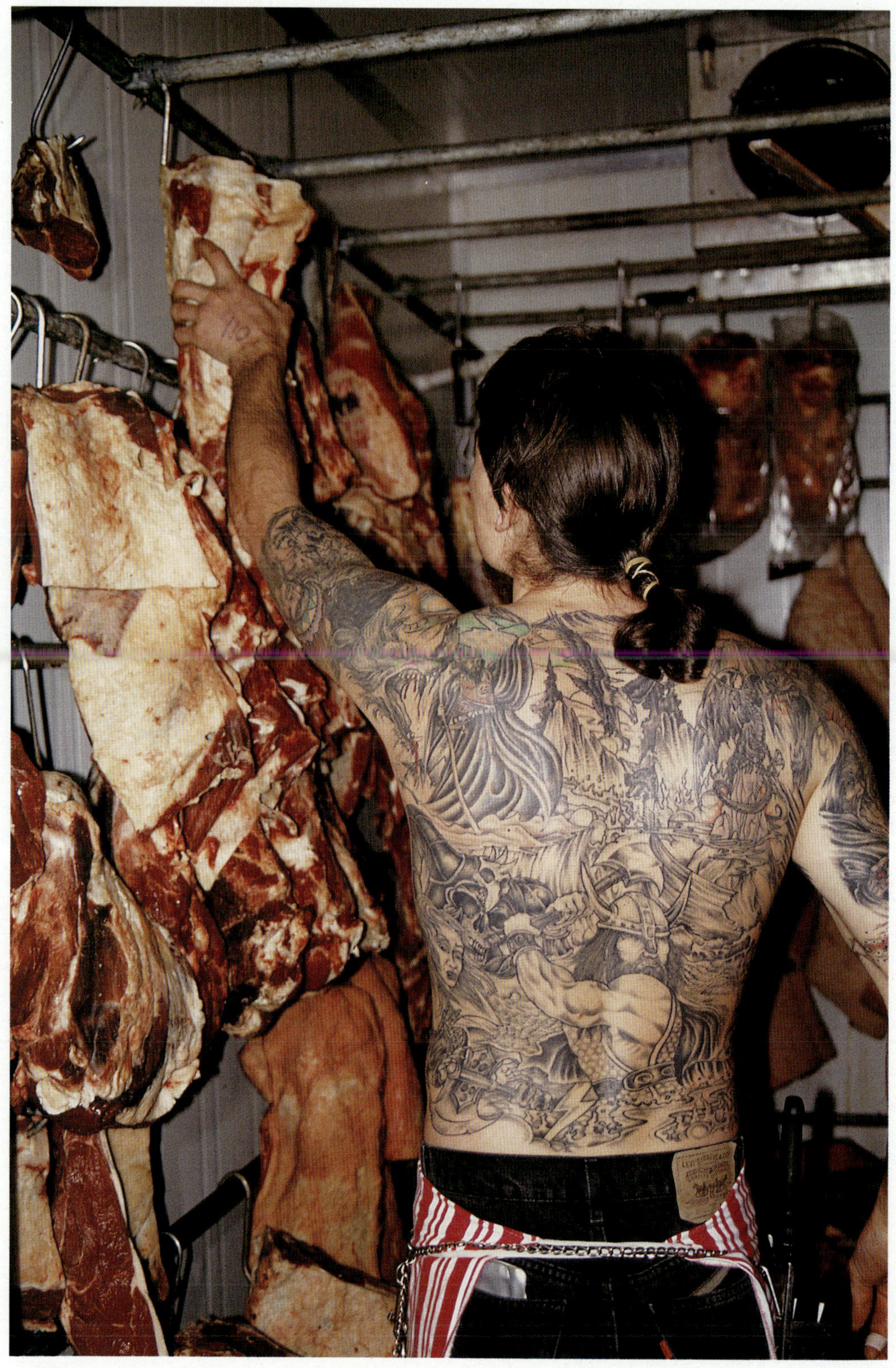

Wayne at work.

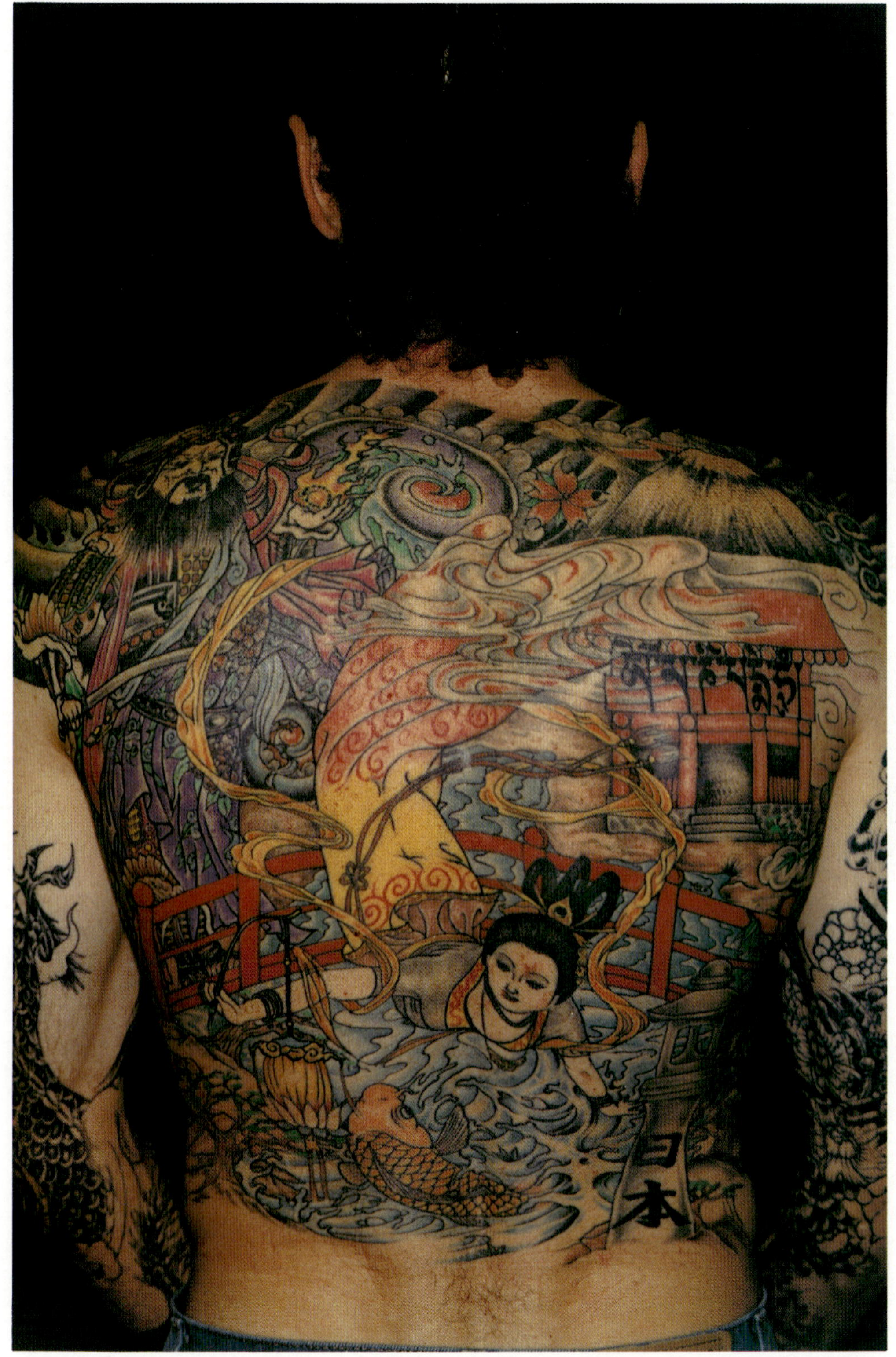

Mark.

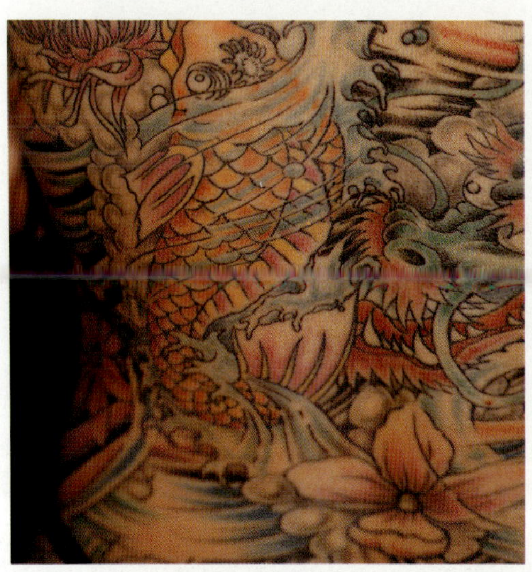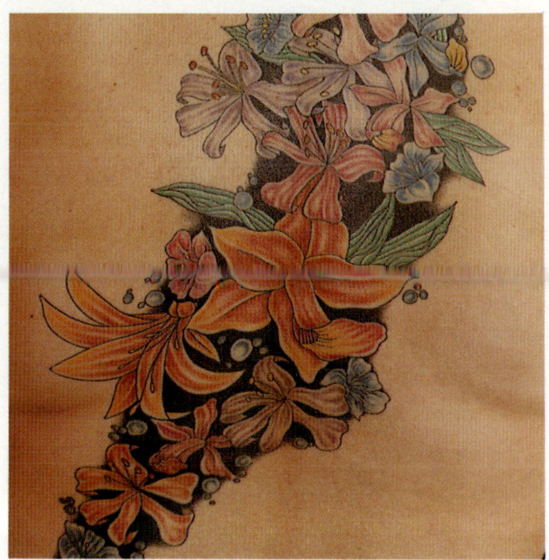

Karen: baby 2 months old at time of photo.

Andrea, tattoo artist

Karen.

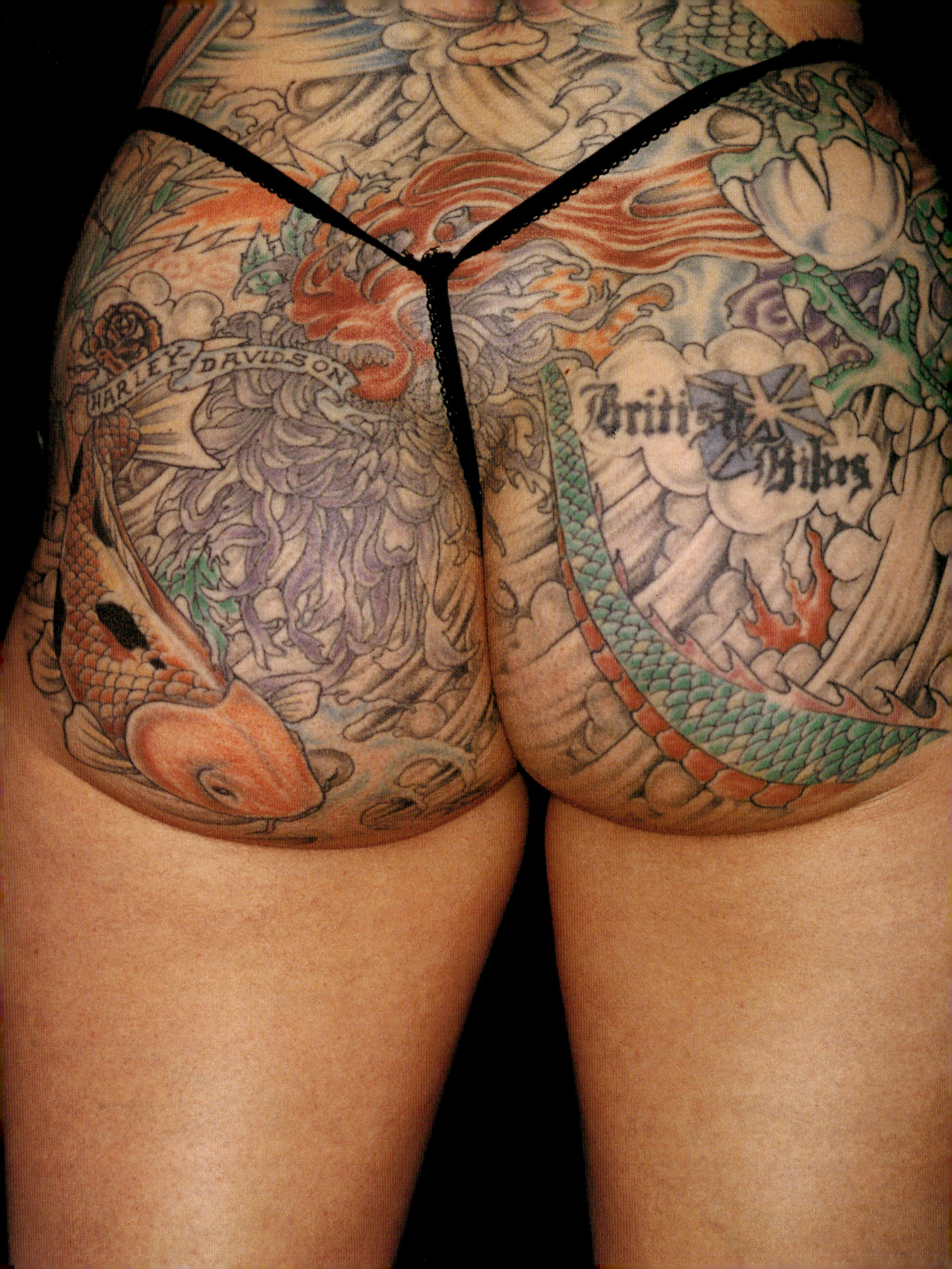
HARLEY DAVIDSON
British Bikes

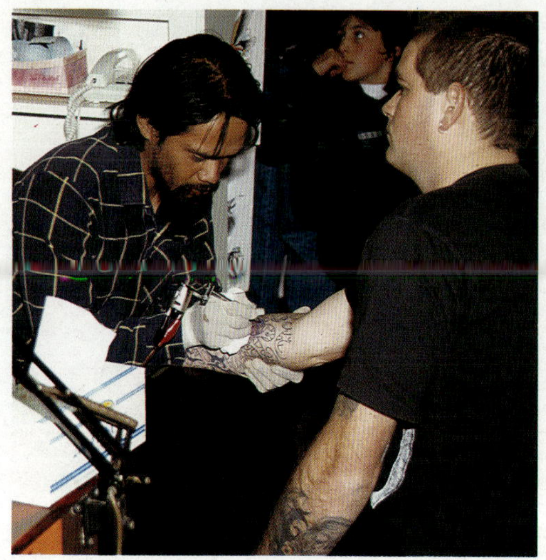

Steve at work.

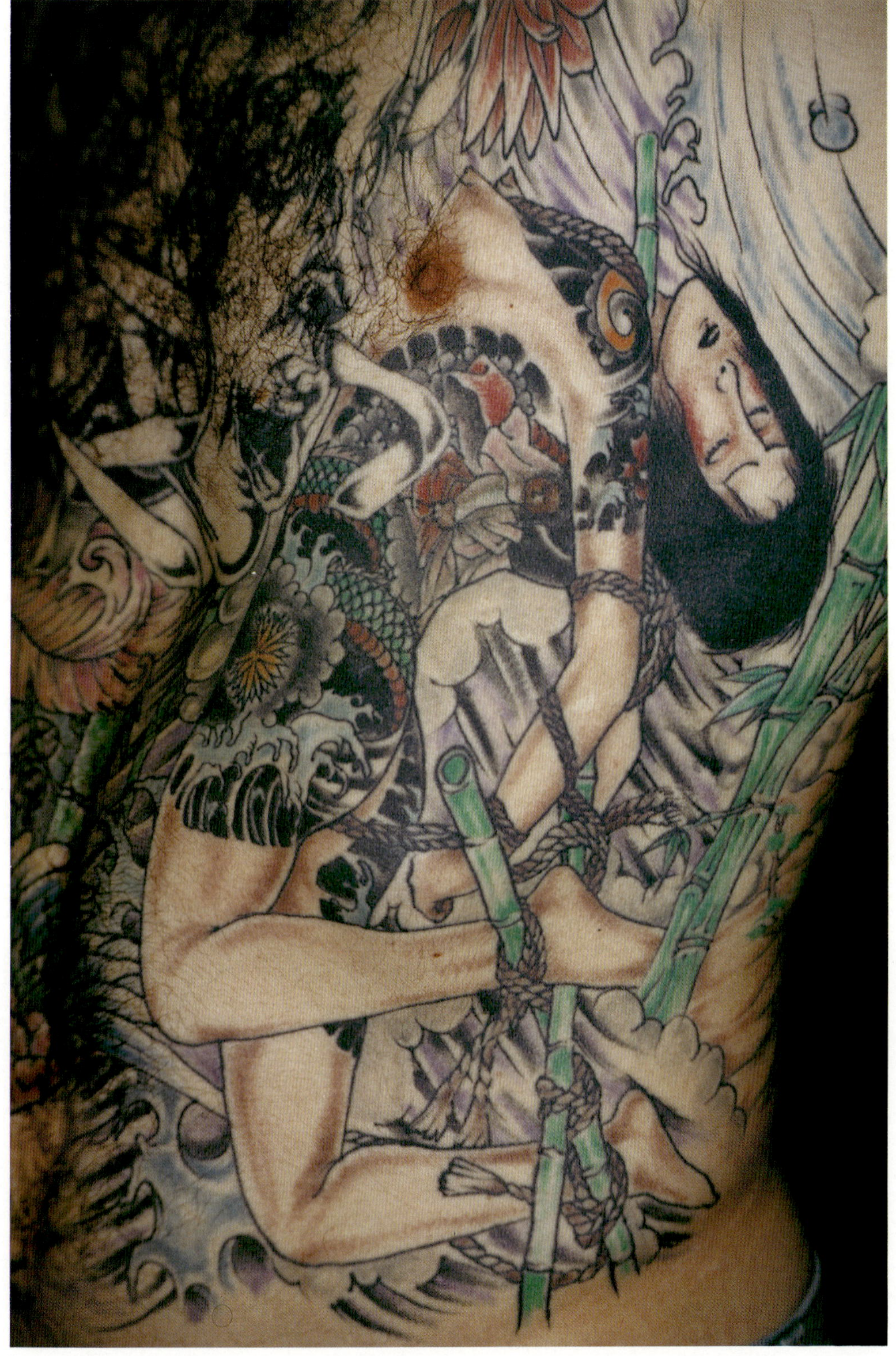

Mark.

# STEVE JOHNSON

STEVE'S PLACE OF BUSINESS is nestled in an industrial area. Tattooing provides workaholic Steve and his family with a lifestyle most only dream of. His studio is small and relatively spartan, but his work is good and people come from all over to get one of Steve's tattoos. Swedish sailors working off the New Zealand coast, in Christchurch on leave with money to spend, arrive in limos to have work done.

America is where Steve looks for inspiration and he visits regularly to catch up with the big names in tattooing and buy the fluoro ink he is famous for. Steve's tattoos glow in the dark! Steve Johnson works in Christchurch.

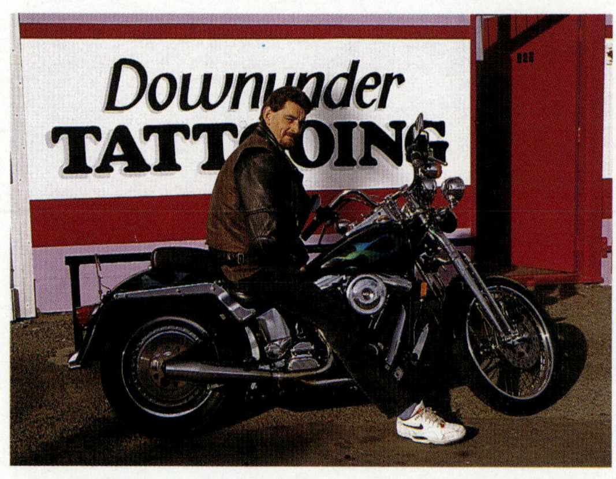


Russell outside the shop.

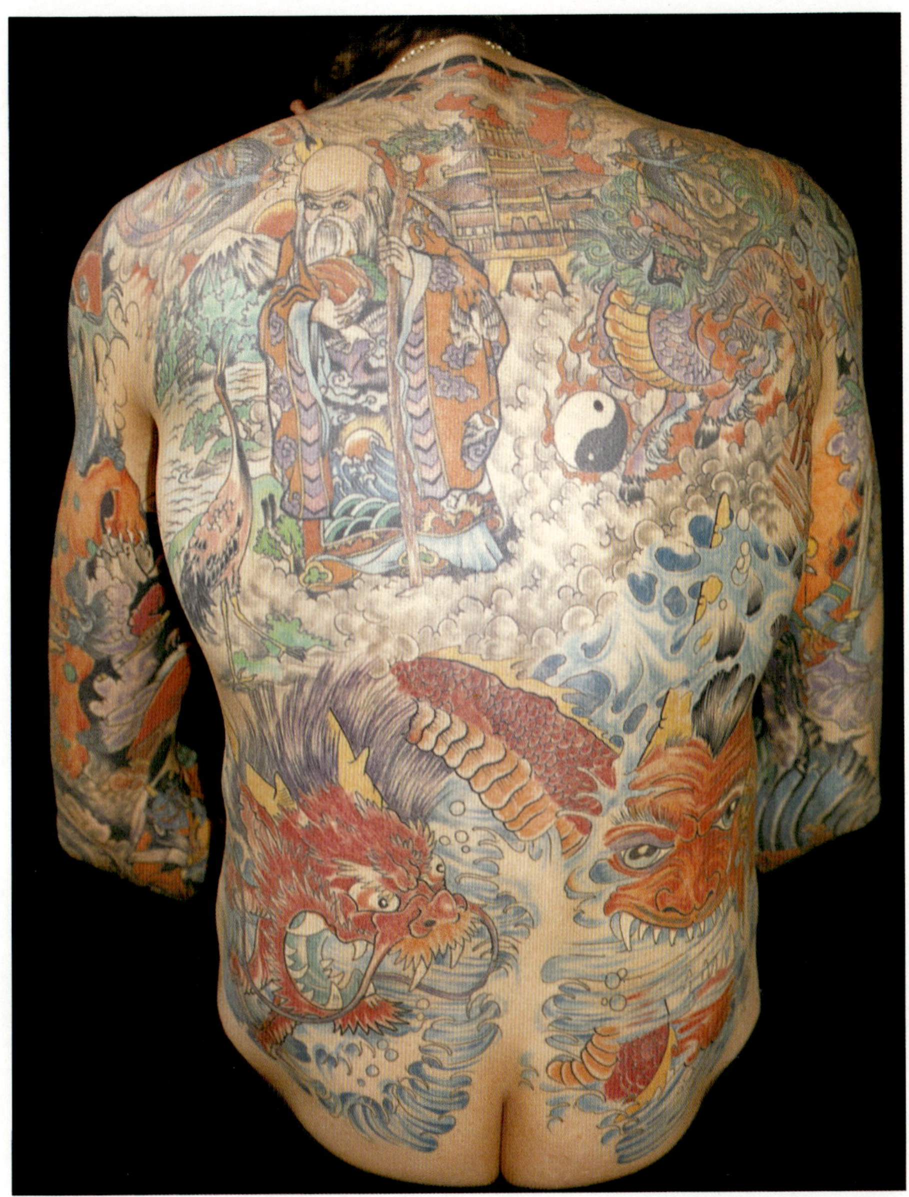

Russell: colours include fluoro ink which
glows in the dark.

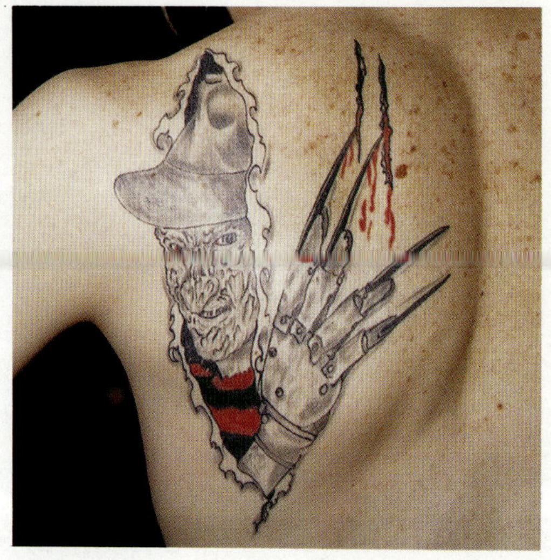

Chris.

Phil: likes bubblegum card type design.

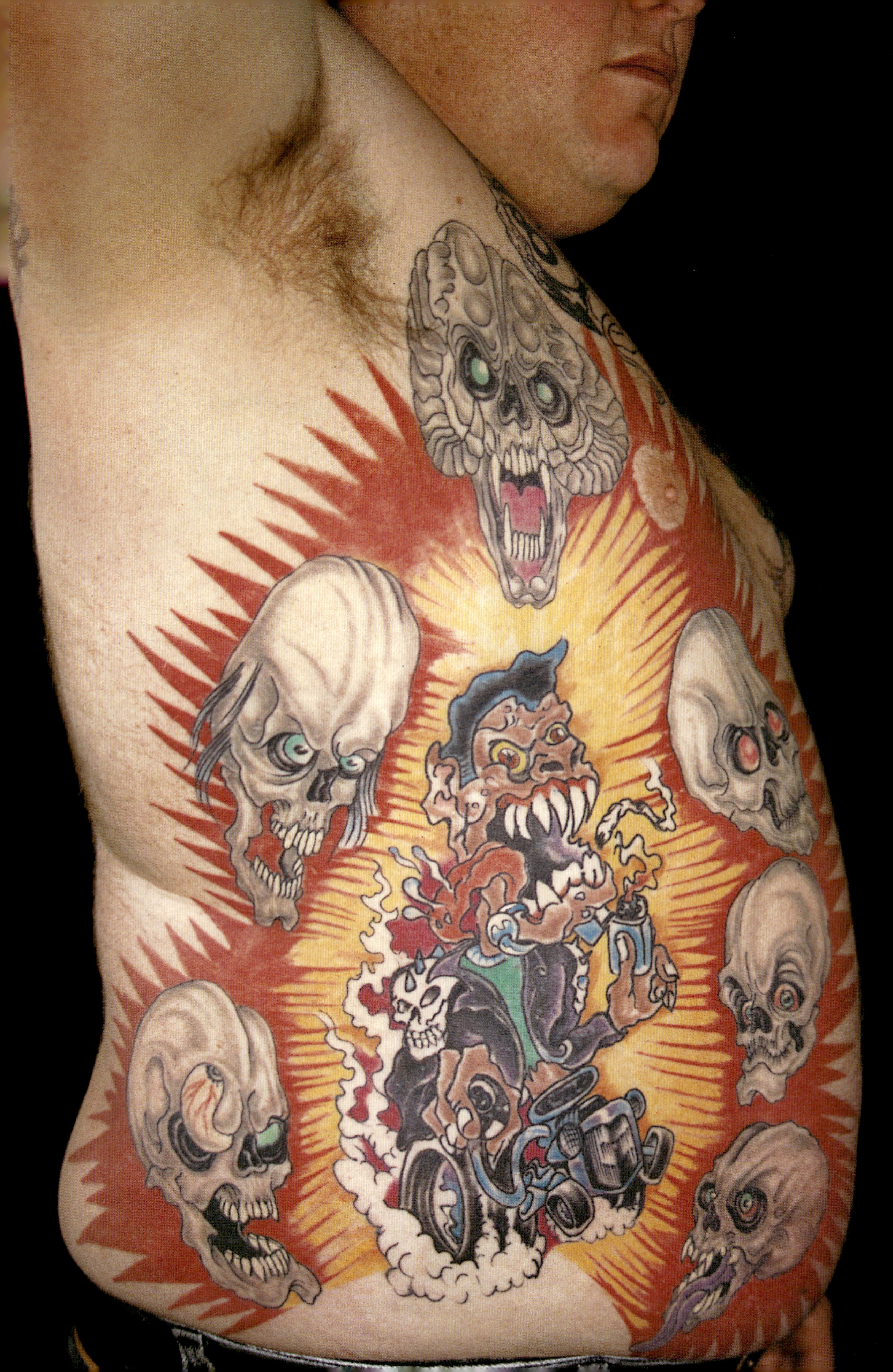

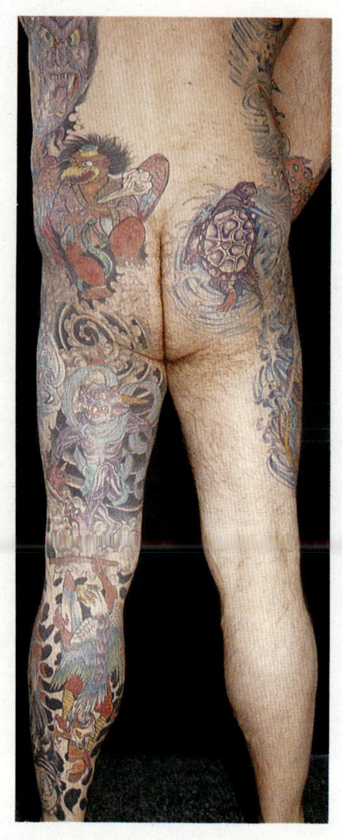

Lester: began getting tattooed 16 years ago.

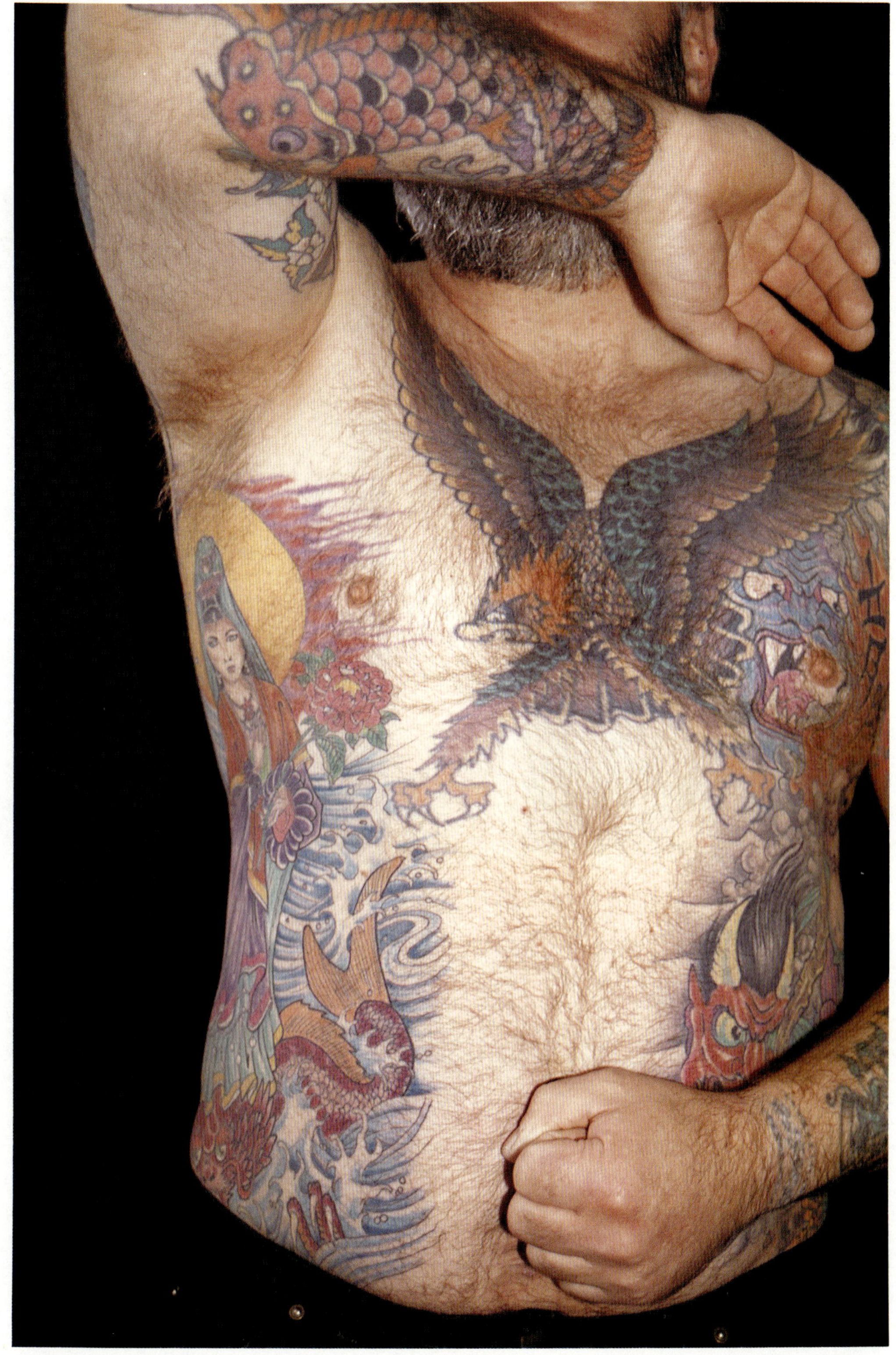

Lester.

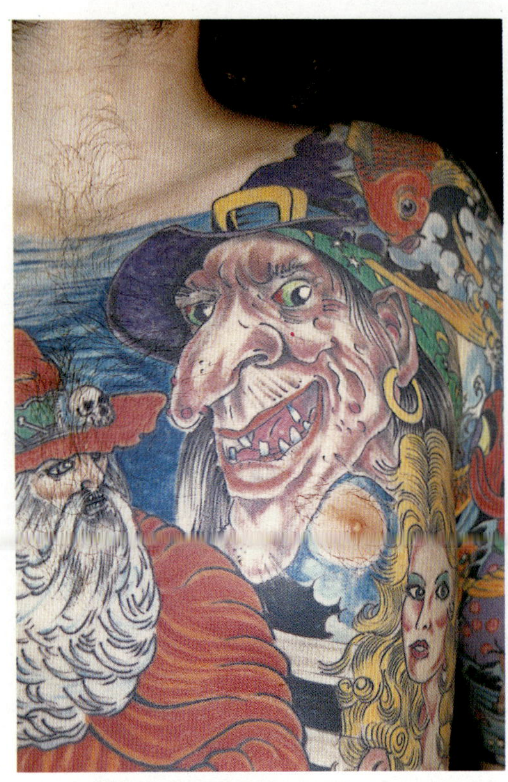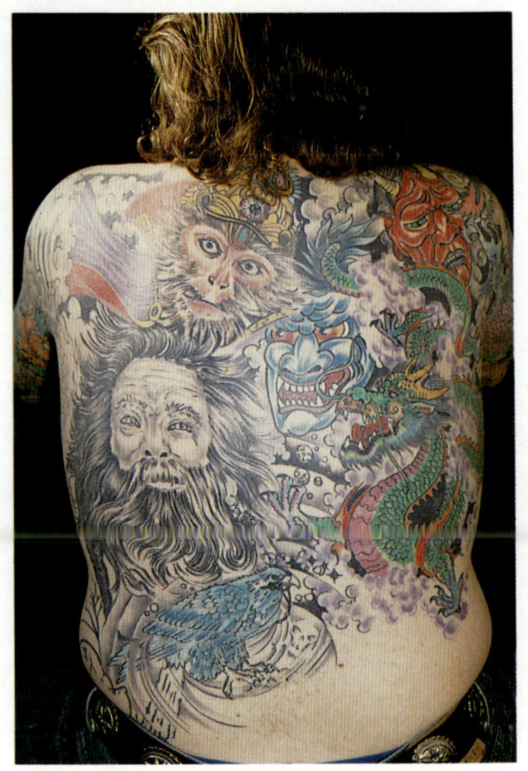

Alan P.

Peter.

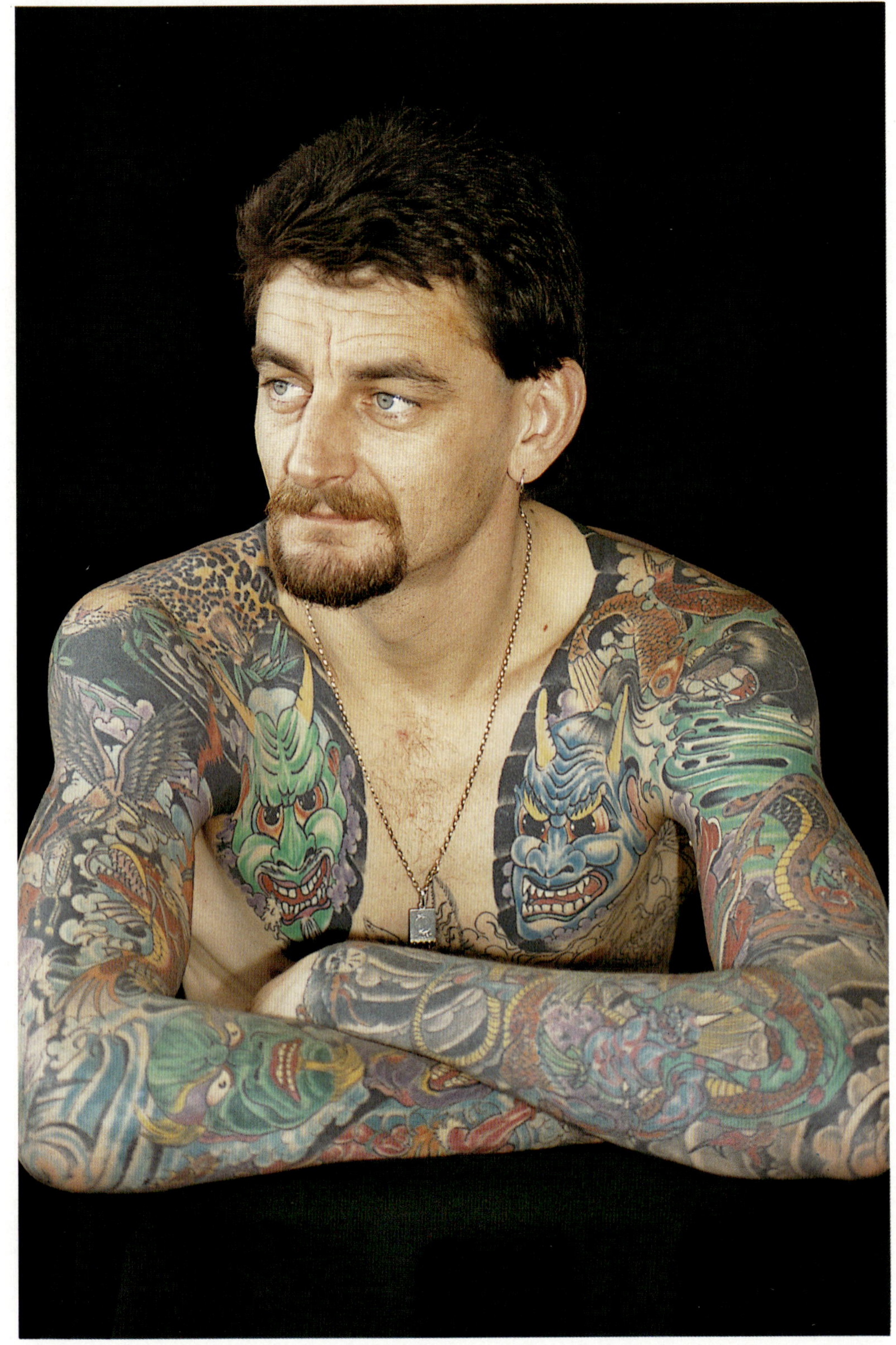

Russell.

# J O H N   D I G G L E

'AWESOME' IS THE WORD I would like to use for the self-portrait on the side of this building. As soon as Digs had completed the mural the landlord increased the rent, because of the improvements to the building. Digs' many loyal clients appeared in force for the photos. Pride of place in the studio is his Harley (you could call this off-street parking). His working area is colourful, with a huge aquarium containing tropical fish. The remaining walls are lined with the best collection of tattoo books I have seen.

Russian sailors off fishing boats visit his studio and trade cigarettes for a downunder tattoo. This man is passionate about animals, which are his favourite subject for tattoos.

John Diggle works in Christchurch.

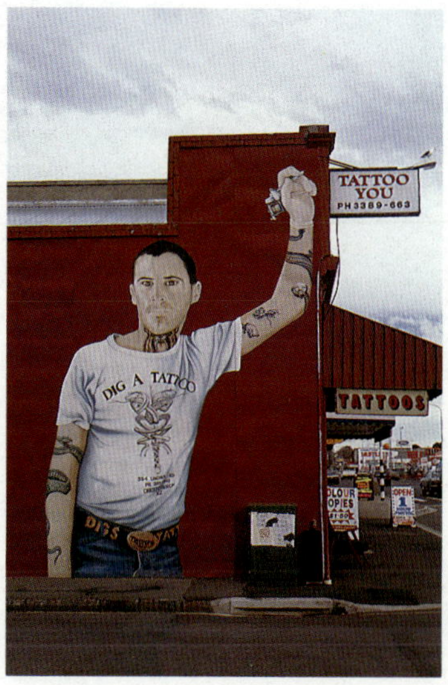


The Shop.

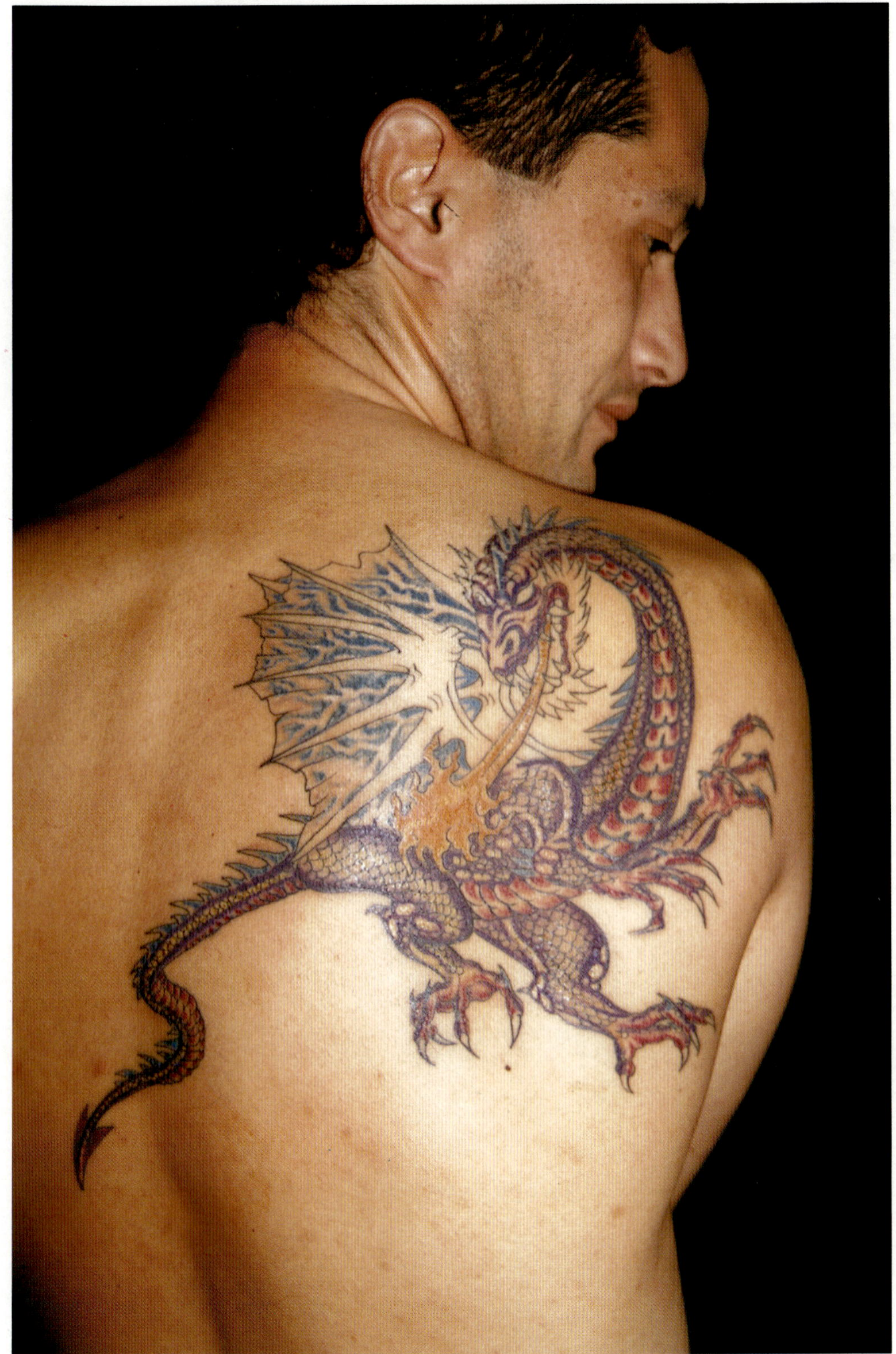

Mark.

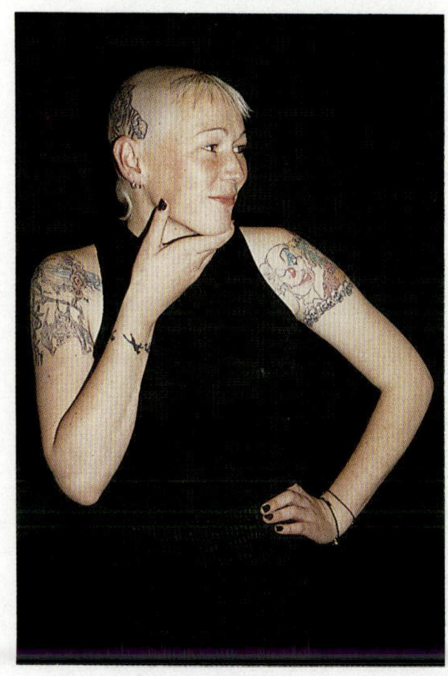 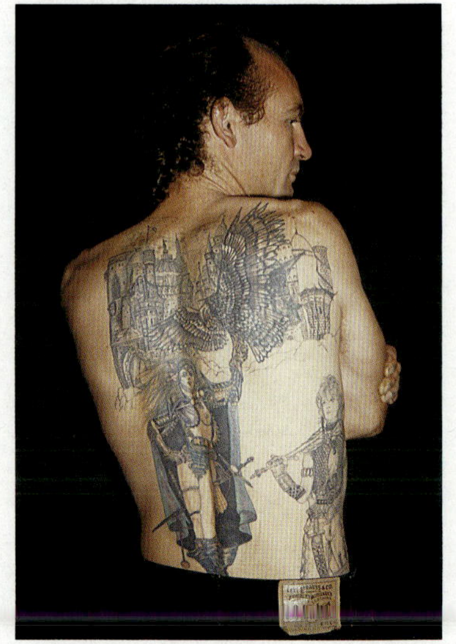

Bobbie

Tony: design inspiration was a book cover.

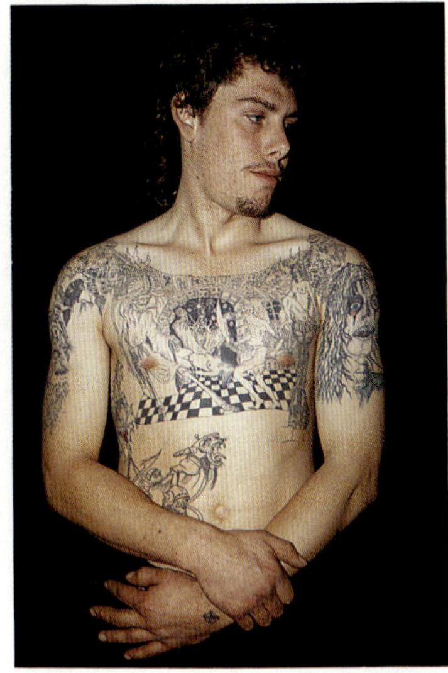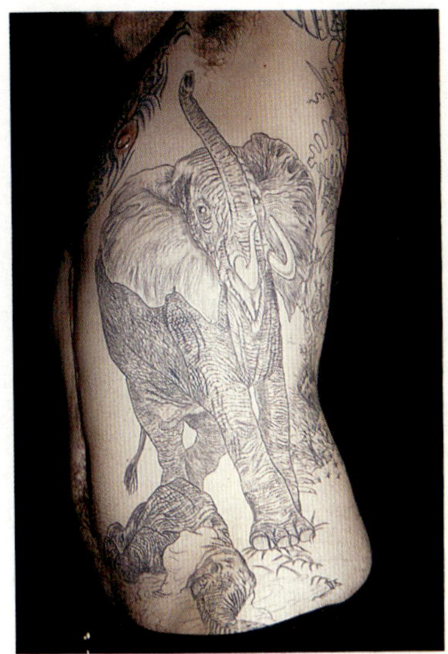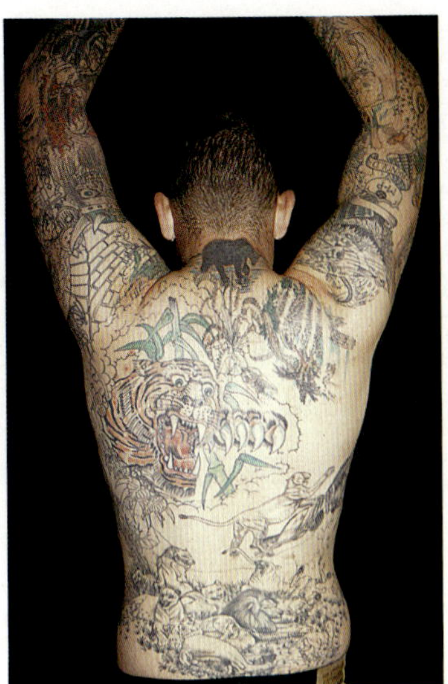

Brian: into fantasy games, started getting tattoos
4 years ago.

Jason: has a great love of animals, many pets at
home.

Jason.

SPACIOUS, LIGHT AND CLINICAL is how I would describe this newly established studio. Clint is a pleasant person with an open, friendly manner. As I was late for the appointment his clients had departed; however, a few quick phone calls soon had them hotfooting it back to the shop to have their photographs taken.

While we waited, Clint made tea, and offered to give me my first tattoo. When I declined his most generous offer, he suggested I choose a very colourful fake one to be worn on a special occasion. Thank you Clint, my mother freaked out at that one.

Clint works in Masterson.

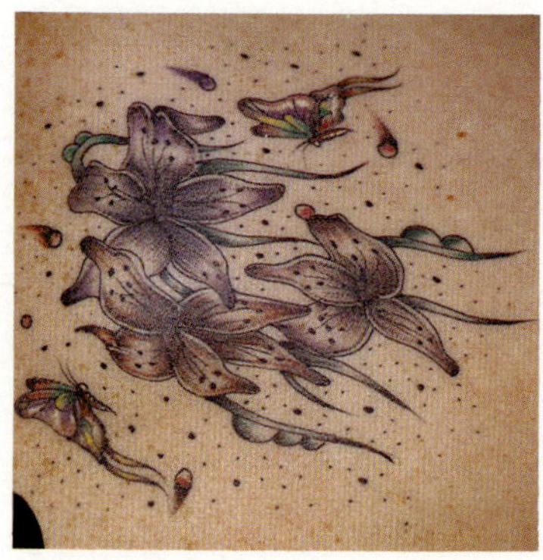

Kathy.

Recard, retired. His first tattoo.

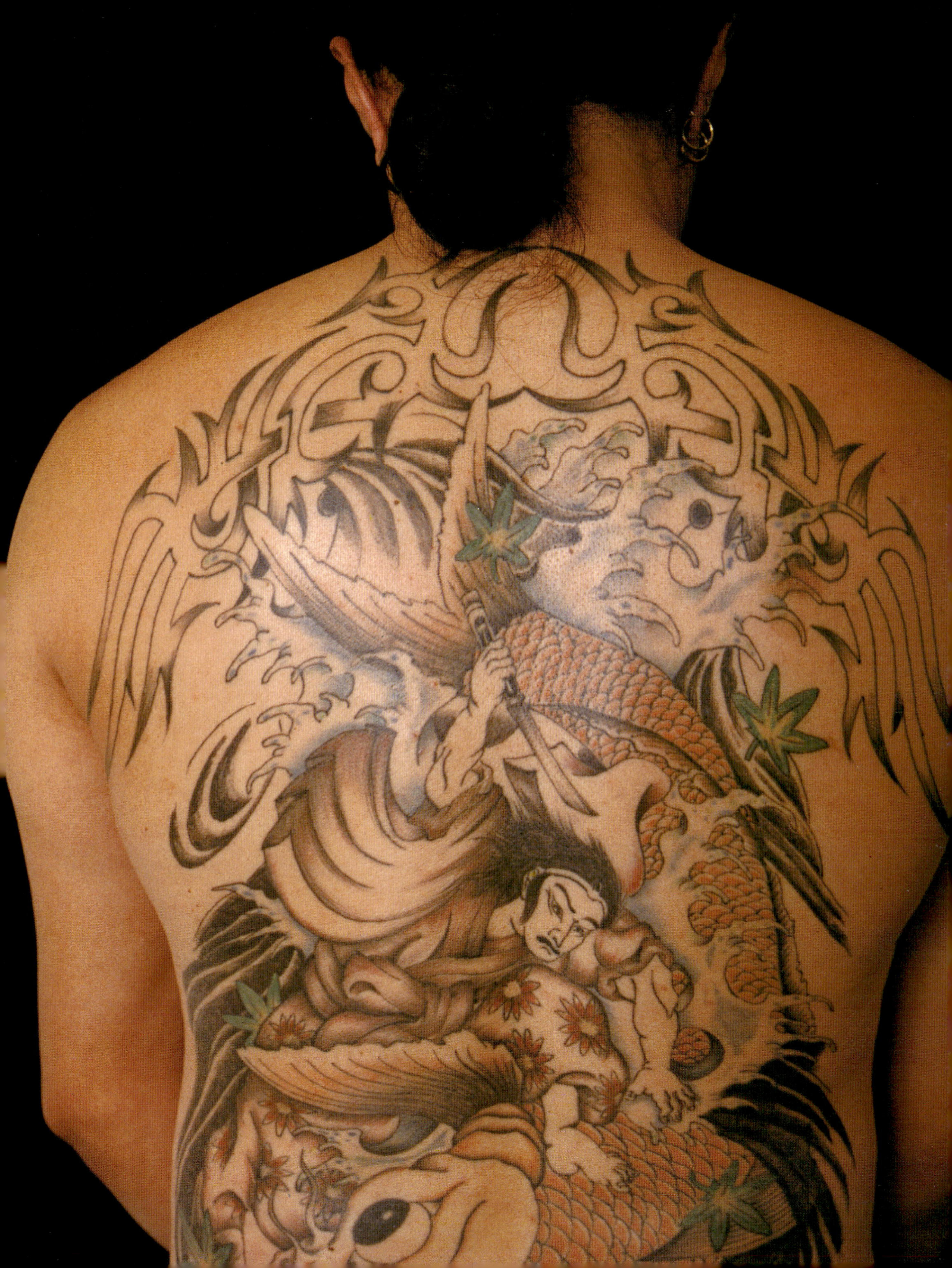

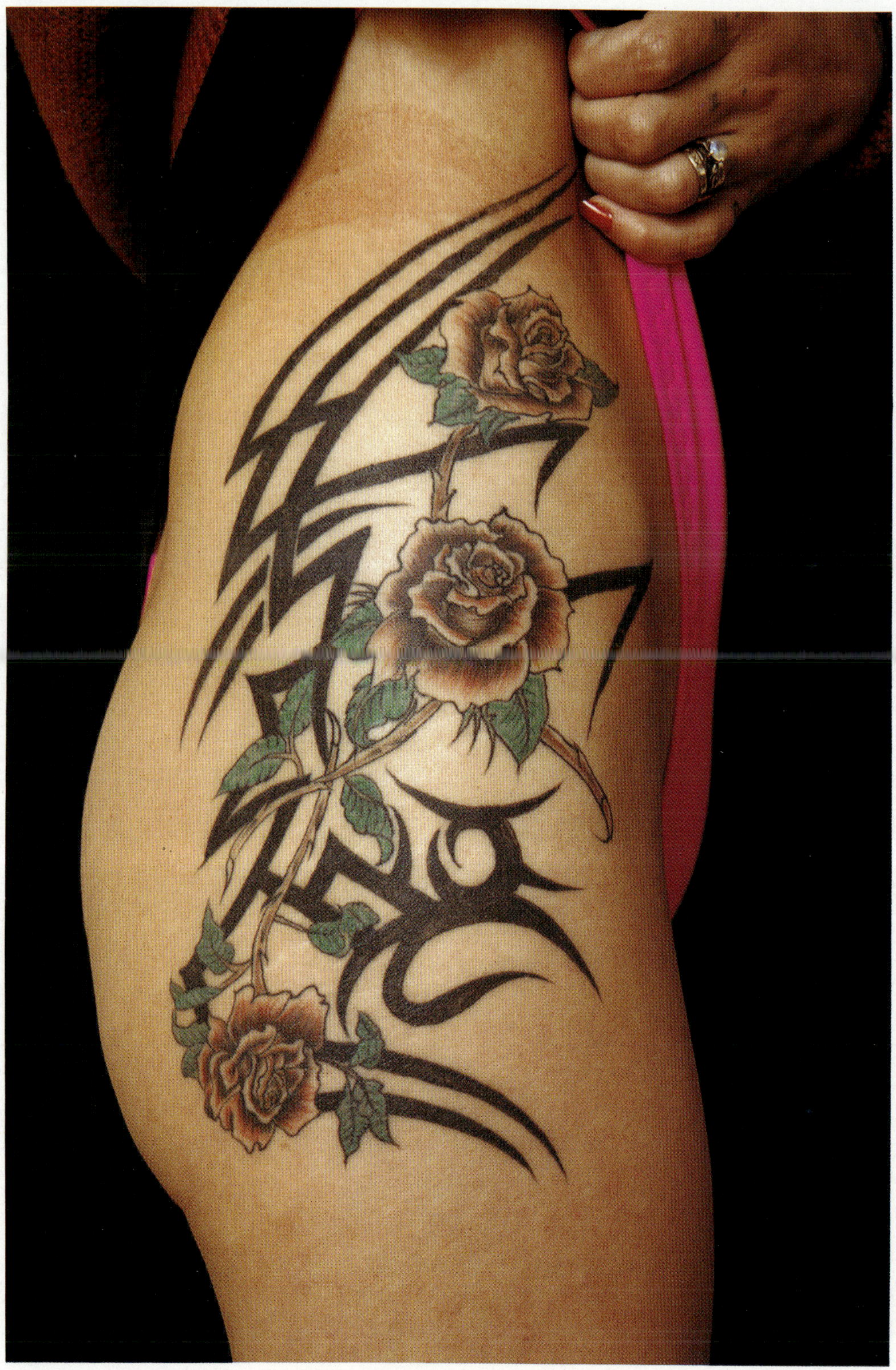

Ngaio.

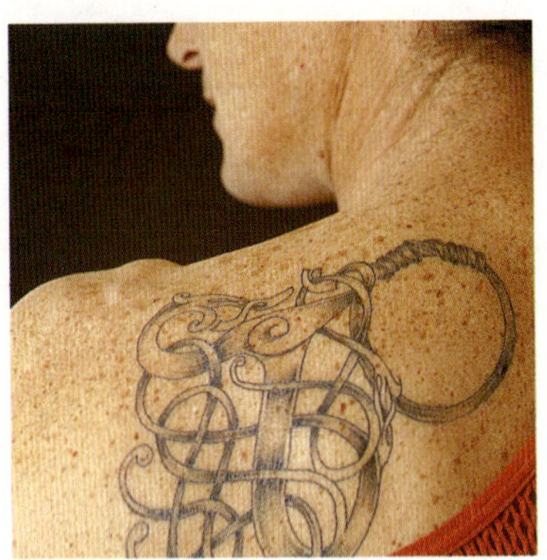 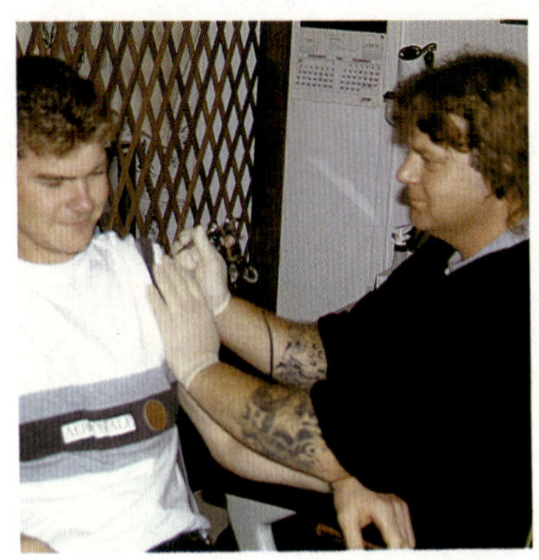

Mark: likes bold designs.

Clint the tattooist.

Ta Moko Moko Tangi (Iwi — Tribe — Ngati Kahungunu)

Semi details *Kaupapa Ngati Kahungunu*

Symbolic References

*1* Loyalty—Trust—Honour

in life and in death, physically and spiritually.

2 Acknowledgement of our Tipuna of the past, of the Kaupapa of our present.

3 Identity of our people (*Ki Te Maori*)

Acknowledgement of spiritual and physical strength.

*Kaitiaki* (Guardian) symbol = Nightwolf.

Forehead *Ihi-*(Spiritual strength)

Forehead *Kaitiaki* (Guardian)

Chin *Mana—Ihi* (Physical strength)

According to the Kaupapa, if the Tamariki or Wahine of the Te Amo are threatened or suffer loss of life at the hands of the offender he will die of an execution rite, by being beheaded.

*Micki Te Amo.*

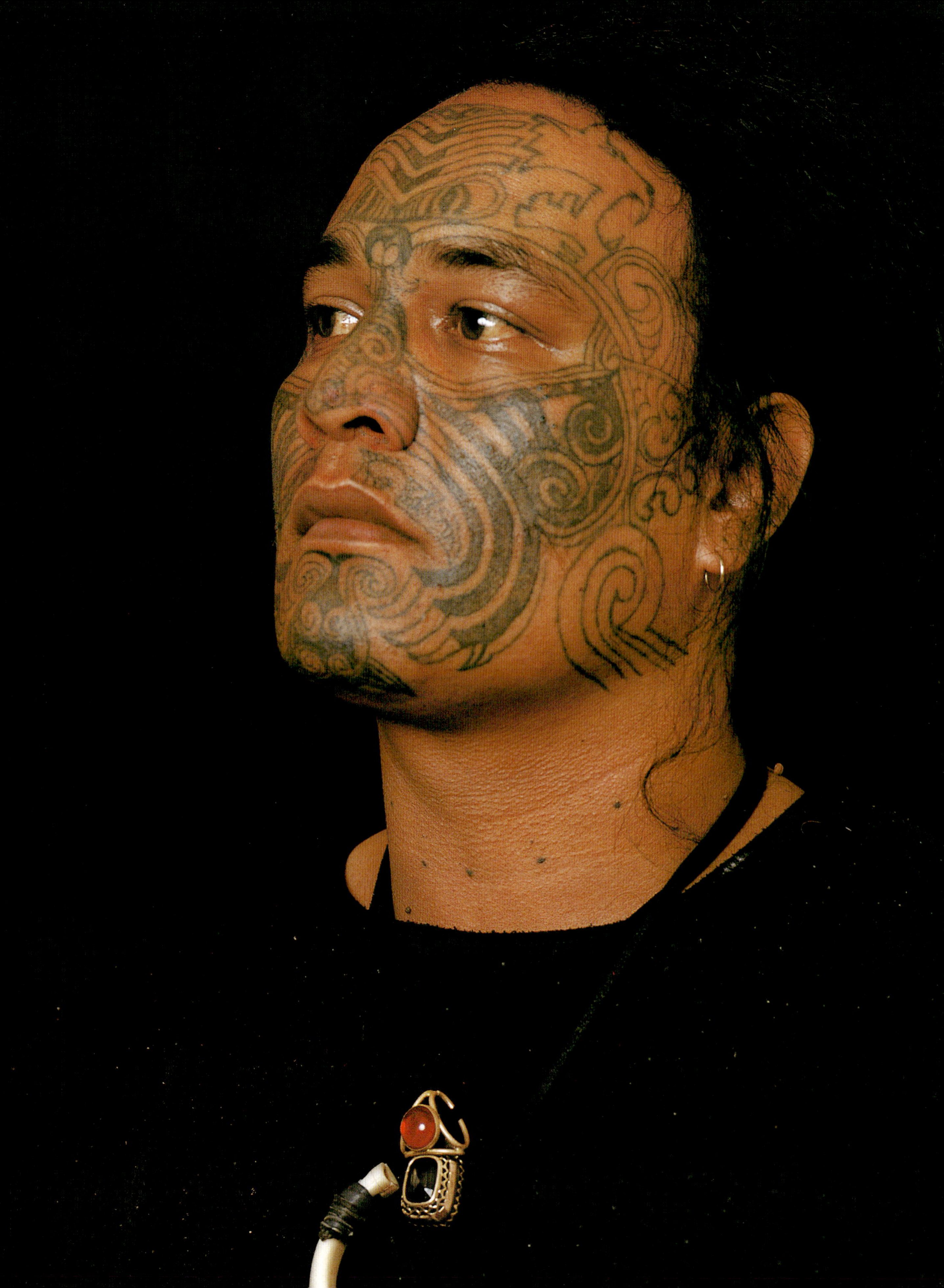

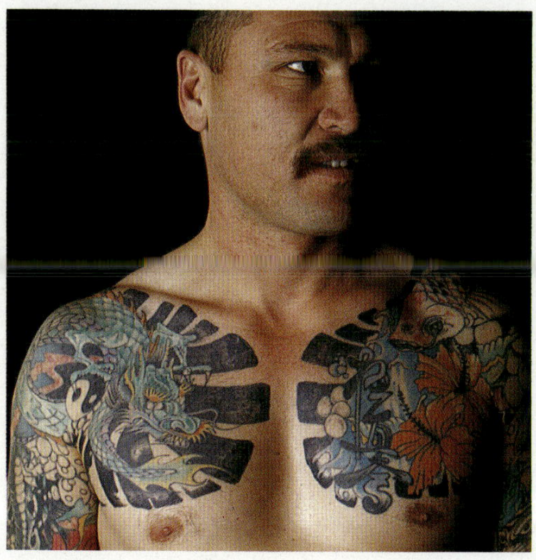

Kevin, police constable.
Tattoos on legs: Paulo Sulu'ape;
Chest: Gypsy; Forearms: Eagle Neil/Ron
Mahon;
Back: Eagle Neil, Merv O'Conner.

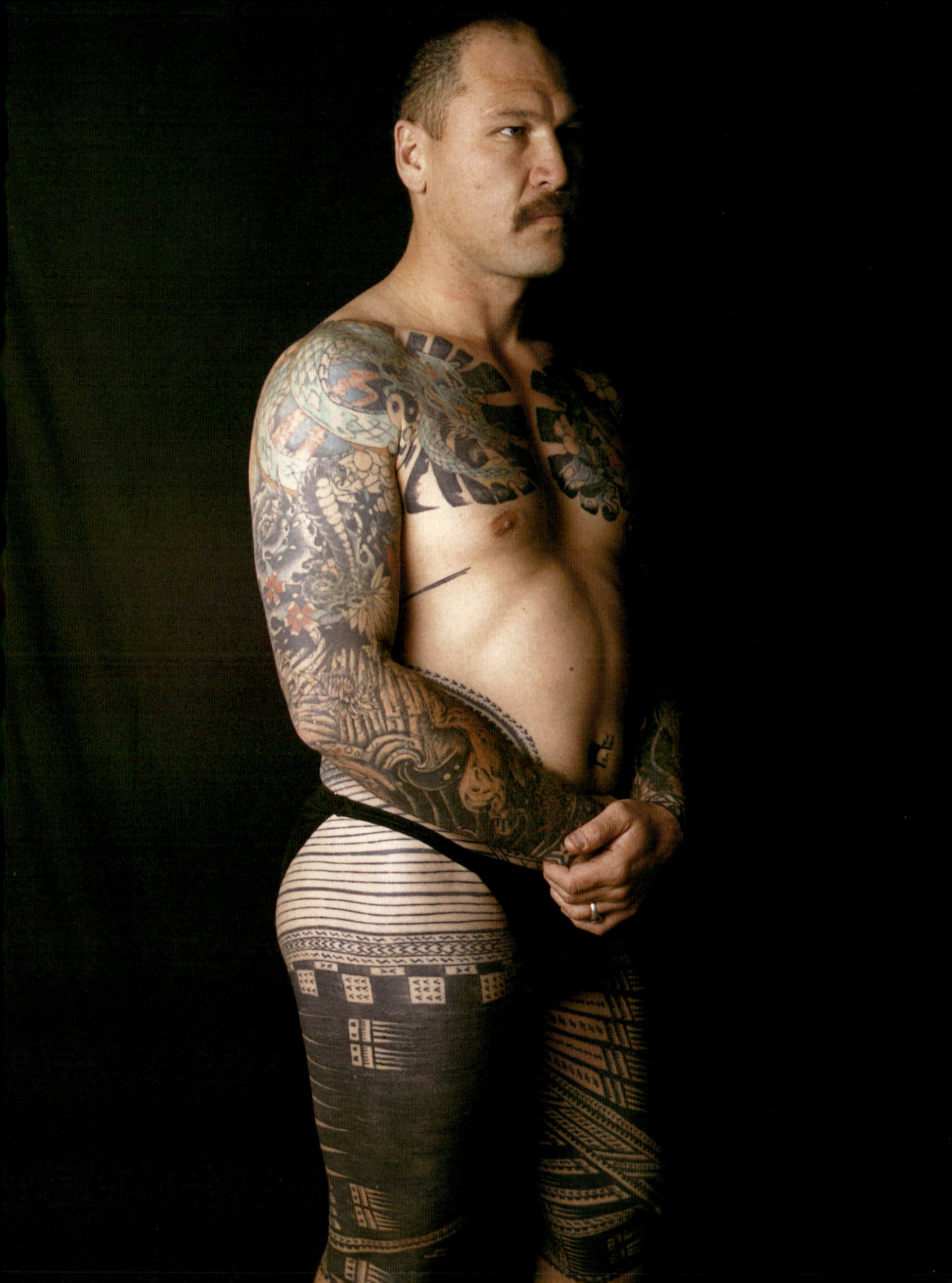

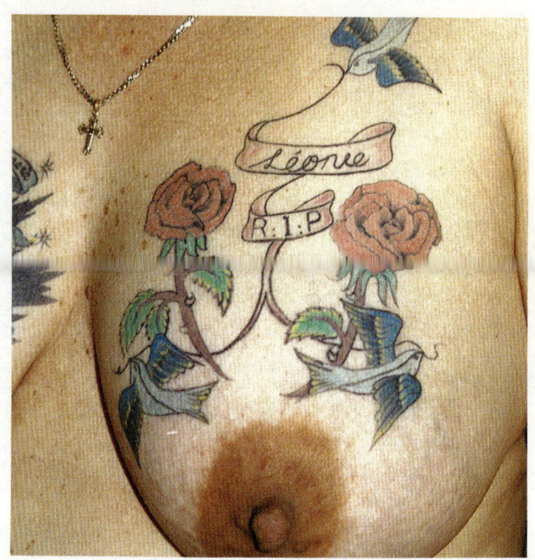

Leigh, Mother.
Tattoo in memory of friend Leonie.


Mad Max, Brett and Ernie, Tattooists.
Photographed at New Plymouth Magog Show
1993.

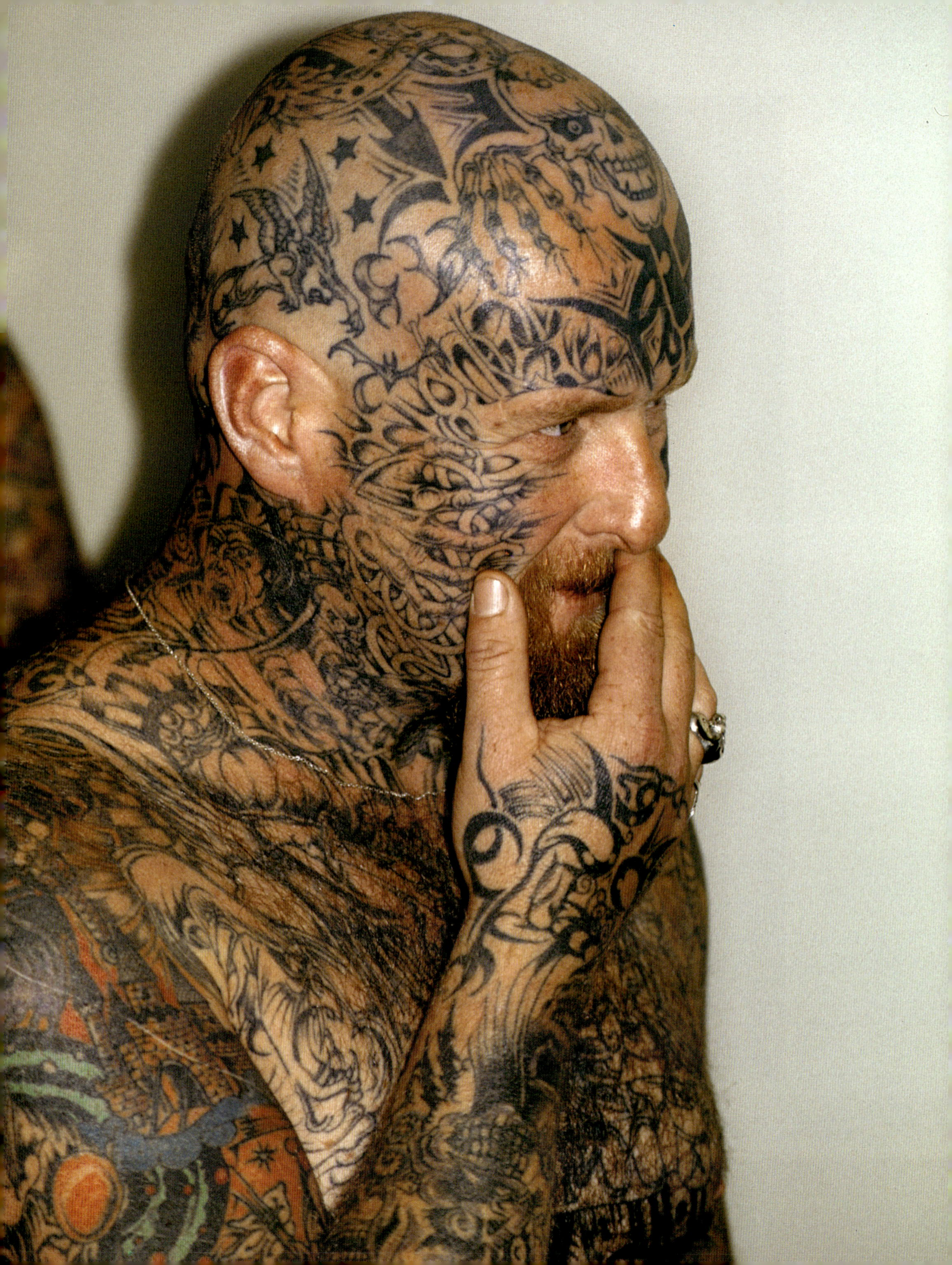

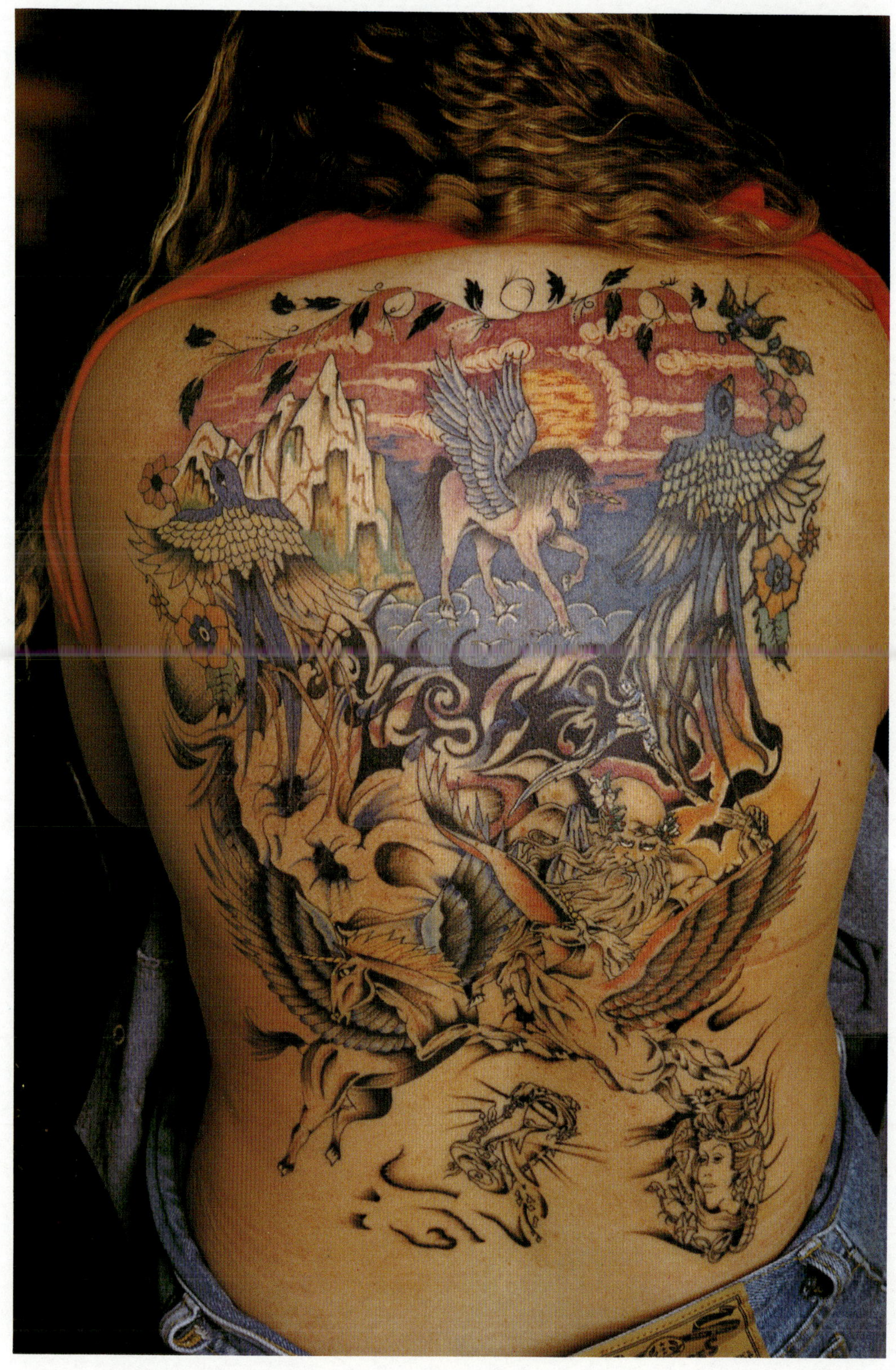

Pauline: tattoo by Tatu.

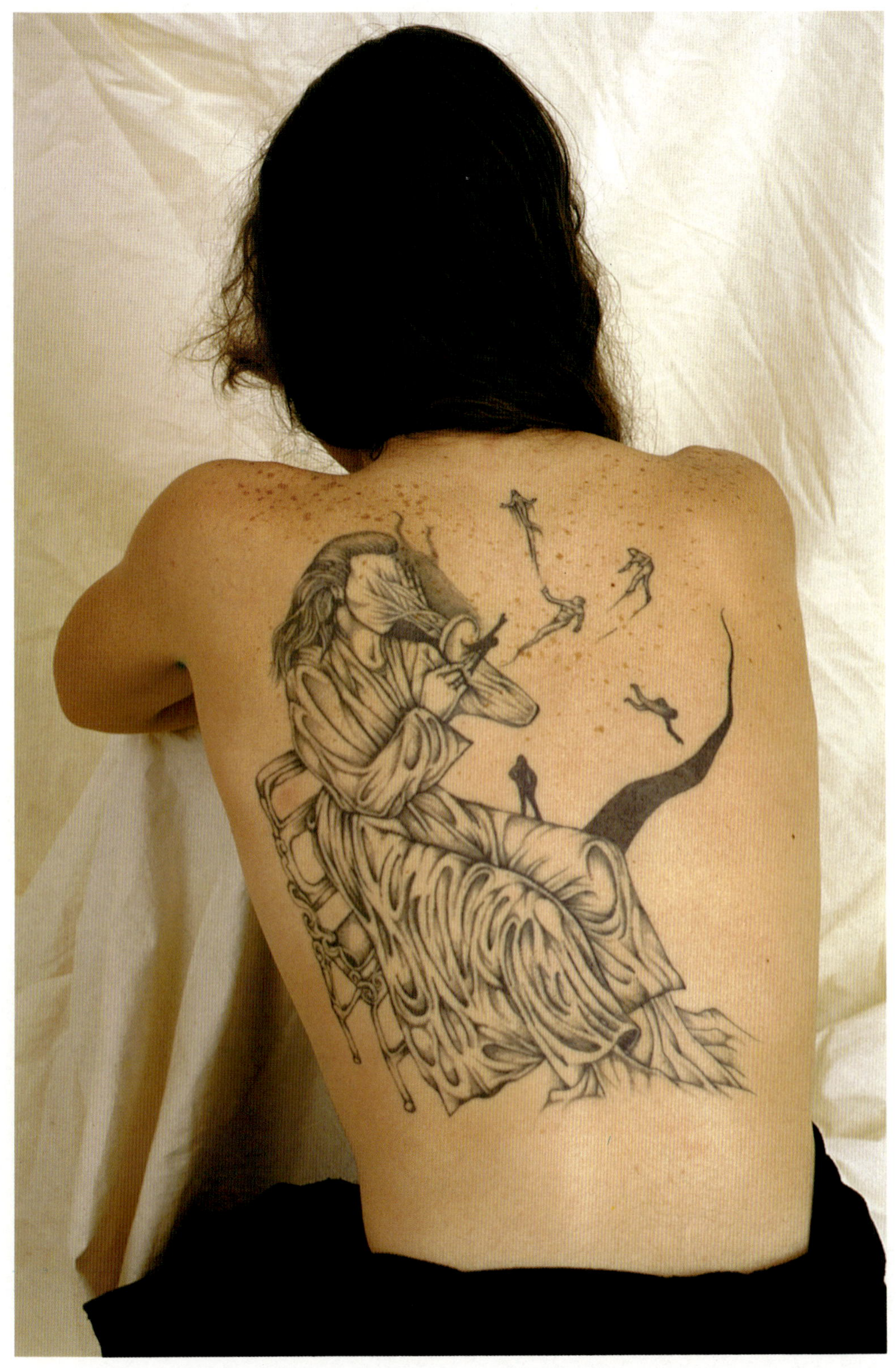

Romelia: tattoo by Brett and Ernie.

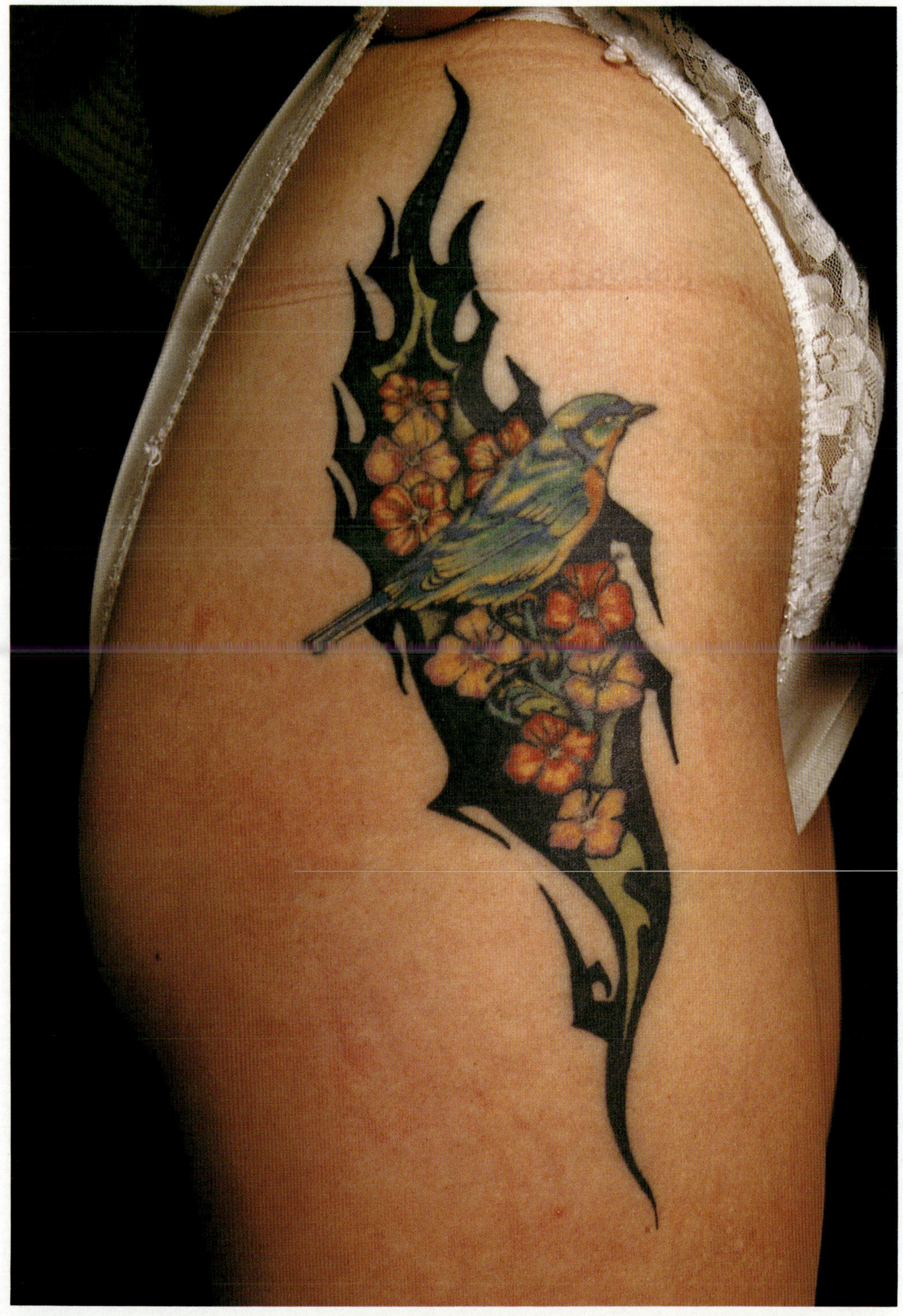

Kay: tattoo by Colan Breed.

Magog Show 1993: tattoo by S.S. (Steve Mormon).

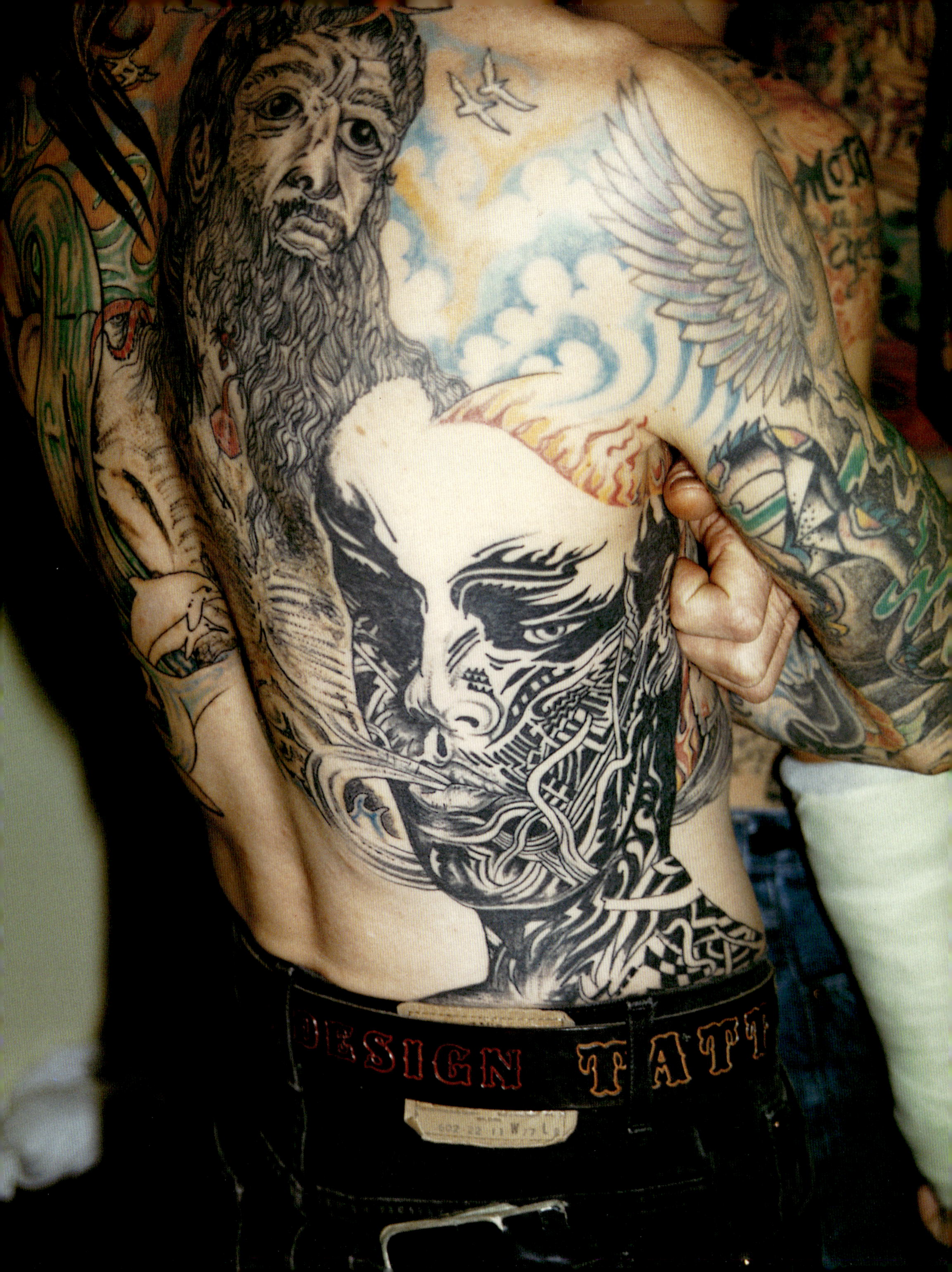
DESIGN TATT

Cameron: tattoos by Tommy Downs / Roger
Ingerton.

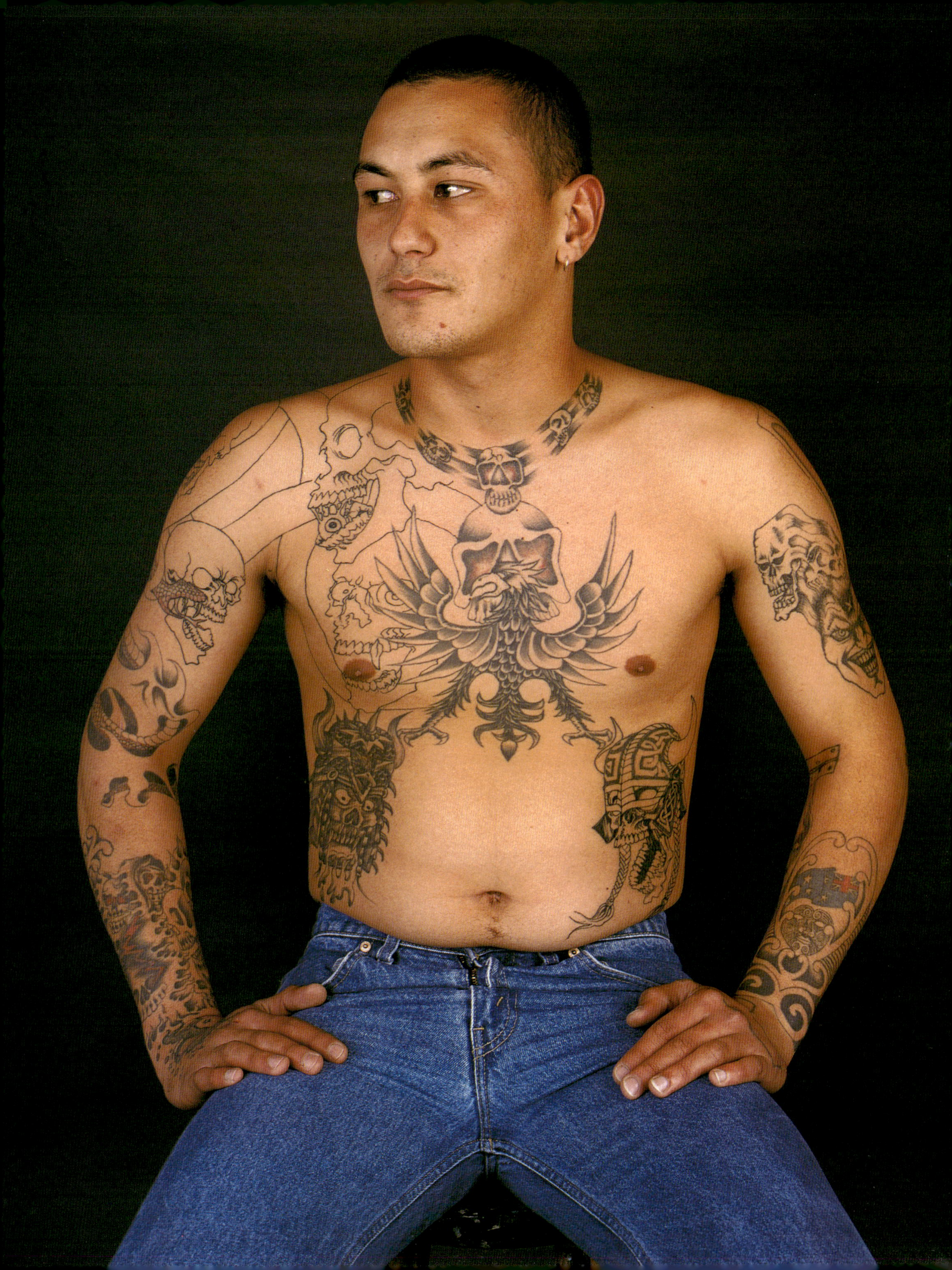

## ACKNOWLEDGEMENTS

Among those people who have helped me in the preparation
of this book, I wish to thank the following:

Daniel Kimi

Greg Taylor

Chris Bezencon

Marion, Cheryl, Katherine and John of Viko Lab.

The Heavily Tattooed Club

Napier Tattoo Club

The tattoo artists and their many co-operative clients.